A.S.A.P. ABSTRACTS PUBLISHING

Physical Education
FLORIDA TEACHER CERTIFICATION EXAM

STUDY GUIDE AND FULL EXAM

BY: Alexandria Lucewich, Masters Public Health
Sharon A. Wynne, MS. Physical Education, Sports
Biomechanics

EDITED BY: Dr. Jerry Holt, PHD and MS in Physical Education

Dedication: This is dedicated to "Doc" Reynolds for giving me the time of day initiating my college education, Prakash for letting me borrow your computer, my mother for her patience and support, and Physical Education Teachers for making a difference in the lives of youths.

TABLE OF CONTENTS

1.0 Knowledge of the history of physical education as a profession   1

2.0 Knowledge of the philosophical basis of physical   6

3.0 Knowledge of sociological aspects of physical education.   9

4.0 Knowledge of psychological implications of physical education.   10

5.0 Knowledge of professional development and involvement.   12

6.0 Knowledge of physical education supervision and management.   15

7.0 Knowledge of legal aspects in teaching physical education.   20

8.0 Knowledge of factors affecting the learning environment.   26

9.0 Knowledge of Physical Education evaluation techniques.   31

10.0 Knowledge of body management components   35

11.0 Knowledge of movement concepts.   37

12.0 Knowledge of mechanical principles of body management.   39

13.0 Knowledge of activities for body management skill development.   48

14.0 Knowledge of the analysis of motor performance.   51

15.0 Knowledge of rules, strategies, and terminology.   52

16.0 Knowledge of appropriate behavior in physical education activities   81

17.0 Knowledge of instructional strategies   82

18.0 Knowledge of physical fitness components.   88

19.0 Knowledge of exercise training principles.   91

20.0 Knowledge of fitness value of activities.   98

21.0 Knowledge of physical fitness program development.   100

22.0 Knowledge of effects of exercise and healthful living on stress.   105

23.0 Knowledge of nutrition and weight control.   107

PHYSICAL EDUCATION

24.0 Knowledge of health risk factors.   114

25.0 Knowledge of the benefits of exercise.   115

26.0 Knowledge of physical fitness issues related to consumers.   129

1.0   Knowledge of the _history_ of physical education as a profession

1.1.   Identify the _contributions_ of early societies to the profession.

Games often had a practical educational aim like playing house. There may also have been political aims such as the gladiatorial games. Economic games included fishing. Families played board games. There were ceremonial reasons for games found in dances. Ball games also provided an opportunity for socialization.

Early society - The common activities performed in early societies included war like games, chariot racing, boating and fishing, equestrian game boards, hunting, music and dancing, boxing and wrestling, bow and arrow activities; dice and knucklebones.

Egyptian - The common activities performed in Egypt were acrobatics, gymnastics, tug of war, hoop and kick games; ball and stick games, juggling, knife throwing games of chance, board games, and guessing games (such as how many fingers are concealed).

Bronze age - The activities performed during the Bronze Age (3000 to 1000 BC) were bullfights, dancing, boxing, hunting, archery, running, and board games.

Greek age - The Greeks are best known for the Olympic games but their other contributions was the pentathlon that included the jump, the discus, and the javelin. The Pankration was a combination of boxing and wrestling. The Greeks played on a see-saw, enjoyed swinging, blind man's bluff, hand guessing games, hoop and board games, and dice games. Losers had to carry their partner's pick-a-back. There also were funeral games in the Iliad.

Romans - The Romans kept slaves and were advocates of "blood sports." Their philosophy was to die well. There were also unemployment games. Roman baths were popular - as were ball games, stuffed feathers, pila trigonalis, follis and balloon or bladder ball. The Capitoline games were held in 86 AD. These union guild athletes were paid for their activities, such as artificial fly fishing. The games that were popular during this period were top spinning, odd and evens, riding a long stick, knucklebones, and hide and seek.

Chinese - The Chinese contributed the following: jujitsu, fighting cocks, race dogs, playing football. In Korea, Japan, and China, children played with toys and lanterns. Common activities included: building snowmen, playing with dolls, making/playing with shadows, flying kites, and fighting kites. Children enjoyed rope walker toys, windmills, turnip lanterns, ring puzzles, playing horse, hopping, jumping, leapfrog, jump rope, seesaw, drawing straws, tag, counting out, blind man's bluff, measure taking, stone throwing, gambling, backgammon, chess, pebble games, dominoes, and playing cards.

1.2   Identify the _major events_ in the history of the profession.

Egypt - The nobility participated in sport dancing, the masses participated in physical skills, and physical training was engaged in for wars.

Cretans - The Cretans emphasized learning to swim.

Spartans and other Greeks - Severe physical training was emphasized and NOT competitive sport.

Athenians - The harmonious development of the body, mind, and spirit was adopted.

Romans - The **worth of physical education** was dignified by the Romans. During the Dark Ages, children learned fitness and horsemanship. The squires learned how to become knights by boxing and fencing. Swimming was also popular. During the Renaissance, the body was developed for health reasons. The Romans **combined the physical and mental** aspects of exercise in their daily routines.

1349-1428 physical education was necessary for a person's total education and was also a means of recreation.

In 1546, Martin Luther viewed Physical Education as a substitute for vice and evil.

Sweden - Ling, in 1839, strove to make Physical Education a **science.**

Colonial Period - Religions denounced play. Pleasures were either banned or frowned upon.

The National Period began in 1823. **After school,** games and sports were available. There was an introduction to **gymnastics and calisthenics.**

Civil War (1860) - This was a period of gymnastics and non-military use of Physical Education. Physical education became **organized.** Schools included Physical Education in their planning, and Physical Education held a respectable status among other subjects. **YMCA's** were founded. Gulick was the Director of Physical Education at New York College, and Dudley Allen Sargent was teaching Physical Education at Harvard.

Depression of 1930s - **Physical fitness movement began.** Bowling was the number one activity. Dance, gymnastics and sports were popular. The Heisman Trophy was first awarded in 1935. After WWII, outdoor pools were common for the average American.

1.3 Recognize major <u>trends</u> since WW2 that have influenced the profession.

WWII Selective Service examinations discovered the poor physical fitness condition of the country's youths. Thus, **physical education classes focused on physical conditioning.**

1942 - President Roosevelt established the **Division of Physical Fitness** run by John B. Kelly (who alerted Roosevelt about the poor fitness levels of youths). This division was dissolved and **placed under the Federal Security Agency** [FSA] with numerous organizations **promoting fitness.** [Under FSA, Frank Lloyd was appointed Chief of the Physical Fitness Division, William Hughs was appointed Chief Consultant, and Dorothy LaSalle was appointed head of the work for women and children.] **After WWII ended, the eagerness for fitness waned.**

1953 - **Kraus-Webber tests** - Of the 4,264 USA participants, fifty-seven percent (57%) failed a general muscular fitness test. Only 8.7% of the Europeans failed. Again, John Kelly alerted the President (Eisenhower) for the **need of a fitness movement.** Eisenhower ordered a **special conference** regarding this, and it was held in **June, 1956.**

1956 - **AAHPER Fitness Conference established the President's Council on Youth Fitness and a President's Citizens Advisory Committee on the Fitness of American Youth.**

Modern dance gave way to contemporary dance. Gymnastics developed new equipment with a higher balance beam. There were trampolines and uneven parallel bars. The Swedish gymnastics boom was over, and ropes and ladders, wands, dumbbells, and Indian clubs were no longer fashionable. Core sports for boys were football, baseball, basketball, and track and field. Core sports for women were basketball, softball, and volleyball.

John F. Kennedy changed President's Citizens Advisory Committee of Fitness of American Youth name to **President's Council on Physical Fitness.**

Lyndon B. Johnson changed the name to **President's Council on Physical Fitness and Sports.**

1972 - **passage of Title IX** of the Educational Amendments Act to ensure that girls and women receive the same rights as boys and men for educational programs, including physical education and athletics.

1970 to Present Trends - Preventative medicine, wellness, physical fitness, and education that is more scholarly, more specialized, and more applicable to all segments of population such as the elderly, handicapped persons, and those out of school.

Organizations (Non-School sports): AAU mid 20th century controlled amateur sports; Little League; North American Baseball Association.

International Amateur Sports: Olympic Governing Committee.

Intercollegiate: National Collegiate Athletic Association (NCAA scholarship in 1954); National Association of Intercollegiate Athletics (NAIA); National Junior College Athletic Association (NJCAA).

Interscholastic Sports: National Federation of State High School Athletic Associations.

Organizations for Girls' and Women's Sports: Athletic and Recreation Federation of College Women (ARFCW); the Women's Board of the U.S. Olympic Committee; National Section of Women's Athletics (NSWA - promoted intercollegiate sports such as US Field Hockey; and Women's International Bowling and established special committees). The Women's Division of NAAF merged its interests in the NSWA of AAHPER and changed its name to National Section for Girls and Women's Sports (NSGWS). **Mel Lockes, chairperson NSGWS 1956, was against intercollegiate athletics for women.** In 1957, NSGWS changed its name to Division of Girls and Women's Sports (DGWS), still a division of AAHPER. Lack of funds hurt DGWS.

Bibliography

Adams, William C. *Foundations of Physical Education, Exercise, and Sport Sciences.* Philadelphia: Lea & Febiger, 1991.

Bucher, Charles A. *Foundations of Physical Education.* 7th ed. St. Louis: Times Mirror/Mosby, 1975.

Bucher, Charles A., and Deborah A. Wuest. *Foundations of Physical Education and Sport.* 10th ed. St. Louis: Times Mirror/Mosby, 1987.

Daughtrey, Greyson, and John B. Woods. *Physical Education and Intramural Programs: Organization and Administration.* 2nd ed. Philadelphia: W. B. Saunders Company, 1976.

Freeman, William S. *Physical Education and Sports in a Changing Society.* 3rd ed. New York: Macmillan, 1987.

Lee, Mable. *A History of Physical Education and Sports in the U.S.A.* New York: John Wiley & Sons, 1983.

Lumpkin, Angela. *Physical Education: A Contemporary Introduction.* St. Louis: Times Mirror/Mosby, 1986.

Van Dalen, Deobold, and Bruce L. Bennett. *A World History of Physical Education.* 2nd ed. Englewood Cliffs, NJ: Prentice-Hall, 1971.

Wuest, Deborah A., and Charles A. Bucher. *Foundations of Physical Education and Sport.* 11th ed. St. Louis: Mosby, 1991.

2.0   Knowledge of the <u>philosophical basis</u> of physical education.

2.1.   Recognize the influence of past and present education philosophies.

<u>Idealism</u> - The **mind** is of highest importance, developed through knowledge. Values exist independently of individuals. One's personality is developed by the contribution of fitness and strength activities. Horace Mann, Wadsworth, Kant, Plato, and Descartes were idealists.

<u>Realism</u> - The "physical world" is **real.** A realist believes in the laws of nature, scientific method, mind and body harmony; religion and philosophy coexist. Physical fitness results in greater productivity, drills are important to the learning process, athletic programs lead to desired social behavior; play and recreation help life adjustment. Aristotle was a realist.

<u>Pragmatism</u> - **Experience** is the key to life. Dynamic experience shapes individuals' truth. Education is child centered. Varied activities presents more meaningful experiences. Activities are socializing. Problem-solving accomplishes learning. John Dewy and Charles Pierce were pragmatists.

<u>Naturalism</u> - This philosophy is **materialistic.** Things that actually exist are found only within the physical realm of nature, and nature is valuable. An individual is more important than society. Learning is accomplished from self-activities. And, activities are more than physical in nature. Play is important. High competition is discouraged. Physical education takes a holistic approach.

<u>Existentialism</u> - Their chief concern is **individualism.** They do not want the individual to conform to society. Individuals need to have their own system of values; promotes freedom of choice, variety of interests. Playing develops creativity and discovering "inner self". Sartre, and Kierkegaard were philosophers believing in extentialism.

<u>Modern Physical Education philosophies</u>, **Humanistic and Eclectic Philosophies** are followed by most schools today. The **Humanistic philosophy is based on the development of individual talents and total fulfillment that encourages total involvement and participation in one's environment.** Self-actualization and self-fulfillment are encouraged. Curricula of the humanistic approach are more student-centered. **The Eclectic approach combines beliefs from different philosophies.** When blended skillfully, the Eclectic approach affords a sound philosophical approach for an individual.

2.2   Identify <u>goals</u> and <u>values</u> for a physical education curriculum with the philosophy they reflect.

<u>Physical/Organic Development Goal</u> (Realism philosophy) - activities build physical power by strengthening the body's systems resulting in the ability to sustain adaptive effort, quicker recovery time, and resistance to fatigue. **This value is based on an individual being healthier, more active, and performing better by an adequately developed and properly functioning body.**

<u>Motor/Neuromuscular Development Goal</u> (Realism philosophy) - develops body awareness producing movement that is proficient, graceful, and aesthetic that uses as little energy as possible. As many skills as possible are developed so one's interests are

6

wide and varied to allow more enjoyment and better adjustment to group situations. Motor development varied skills affects health by influencing how leisure time is spent. **Values include reducing energy expenditure, building confidence, bringing recognition, enhancing physical and mental health, making participation safer, and contributing to aesthetic sense.**

<u>Cognitive Development Goal</u> (Idealism philosophy) - deals with acquiring knowledge and ability to think and interpret the knowledge. Time, space, and flow of movement are related to scientific principles. Learning physical activities requires thinking and coordination of movement and mastering and adapting to one's environment. Individuals also should acquire knowledge of rules, techniques, and strategies of activities. **Cognitive values include healthy attitudes and habits such as body awareness, importance of personal hygiene, disease prevention, importance of exercise, proper nutrition, and knowledge of health service providers.**

<u>Social/Emotional/Affective Development Goal</u> (Existentialism philosophy) - deals with helping individuals make adjustments - personal, group, and societal by positively influencing human behavior. Success is based on performance, and success develops self-confidence. An appropriate self-concept is important and is accomplished by wholesome attitudes throughout the various growth stages. **Values include meeting basic social needs (sense of belonging, recognition, self-respect, and love) that produces a socially, well-adjusted individual.**

6

Bibliography

6

Bucher, Charles A. *Foundations of Physical Education.* 7th ed. St. Louis: Times Mirror/Mosby, 1975.

Bucher, Charles S. A, and Deborah A. Wuest. *Foundations of Physical Education and Sport.* 10th ed. St. Louis: Times Mirror/Mosby, 1987.

Van Dalen, Deobold, and Bruce L. Bennett. *A World History of Physical Education.* 2nd ed. Englewood Cliffs, NJ: Prentice-Hall, 1971.

Wuest, Deborah A., and Charles A. Bucher. *Foundations of Physical Education and Sport.* 11th ed. St. Louis: Mosby, 1991.

3.0   Knowledge of sociological aspects of physical education.

3.1   Identify the <u>social skills</u> and values from participation in physical activities.

Social skills and values gained from participation in physical activities include the following:

- The ability to make adjustments to both self and others by an integration of the individual to society and the environment.

- The ability to make judgments in a group situation.

- Learning to communicate with others and be cooperative.

- The development of the social phases of personality, attitudes, and values in order to become a functioning member of society, such as being considerate.

- The development of a sense of belonging and acceptance by society.

- The development of positive personality traits.

- Learning for constructive use of leisure time.

- A development of attitude that reflects good moral character.

- Respect of school rules and property.

3.2   Identify <u>activities</u> that enhance socialization.

At the junior high level students indicate a desire to play on a team. They also want to learn activities that would prove useful in their leisure hours.

Senior high level students desire to play harmoniously with others and to participate in team play. Students view activities such as dance and sports as a place to learn respect for their fellow students. Physical education classes provides opportunities for enhanced socialization and a change of pace from academic offerings.

Basketball, baseball, football, soccer, and volleyball are social, team activities. Tennis and golf are social activities that are useful in leisure hours.

Bibliography

Bucher, Charles A. *Foundations of Physical Education.* 7th ed. St. Louis: Times Mirror/Mosby, 1975.

Bucher, Charles A., and Deborah A. Wuest. *Foundations of Physical Education and Sport.* 10th ed. St. Louis: Times Mirror/Mosby.

Wuest, Deborah A., and Charles A. Bucher. *Foundations of Physical Education and Sport.* 11th ed. St. Louis: Mosby, 1991.

8

4.0 Knowledge of psychological implications of physical education.

4.1. Identify the positive and negative influences of participation in physical activity on psycho-social factors.

Positive Individual Influences:

Feeling better, reduces tension and depression, means of affiliation with others, offers exhilarating experiences, aesthetic experiences, positive body image, controls aggression, relaxation and a change of pace from long hours of work, study, or stresses; provides challenge and sense of accomplishment; provides a way to be healthy and fit, improves self-esteem by mastering skills, provides creative experiences.

Positive Group Influences:

Cooperation, acceptance of all persons regardless of race, creed or origin, respect for others, assimilate the group attitude, encouragement, develop relationship of self to a group, develop spirit of fairness, developing traits of good citizenship, developing leadership and followership qualities; self-discipline, provides additional avenues for social acquaintances, social poise and self-understanding; social consciousness with an accompanying sense of values; individual and social development.

Negative influences: ego-centered athletes, winning at all costs, false values, harmful pressures, loss of identity, role conflict; aggression and violence, compulsiveness, over-competitiveness, addiction to exercise (where commitment to exercise has a higher priority than commitments to family, interpersonal relationships, work, and medical advice), escape or avoidance of problems, exacerbation of anorexia nervosa and other eating disorders, exercise deprivation effects, fatigue, overexertion, poor eating habits, self-centeredness; preoccupation with fitness, diet, and body image.

Bibliography

Adams, William C. *Foundations of Physical Education, Exercise, and Sport Sciences.* Philadelphia: Lea & Febiger, 1991.

American Alliance for Health, Physical Education, Recreation and Dance. *Basic Stuff Series I & II.* Reston, VA: American Alliance for Health, Physical Education, Recreation and Dance, 1987.

Bucher, Charles A., and Deborah A. Wuest. *Foundations of Physical Education and Sport.* 10th ed. St. Louis: Times Mirror/Mosby.

Wuest, Deborah A., and Charles A. Bucher. *Foundations of Physical Education and Sport.* 11th ed. St. Louis: Mosby, 1991.

5.0   **Knowledge of professional development and involvement.**

    5.1   **Identify physical education <u>professional organizations</u> and activities which promote professional development.**

1.   Amateur Athletic Union - Protects amateur sports from becoming corrupted. Conducts pre-Olympic trials.

2.   AAHPER - Works with legislatures concerning education and research, works with President's Council on Physical Fitness and Sport, influences public opinion. (Various associations that make up the alliance.)

3.   American College of Sports Medicine - Promotes scientific studies of sports, research, and post-graduate work.

4.   Association of Intercollegiate Athletics for Women (AIWA) - Since NCAA incorporated women's sports, the numbers of AIWA dropped in 1982 and is currently defunct.

5.   Canadian Association for HER.

6.   Delta Psi Kappa.

7.   National Association for PE for College Women (also includes men).

8.   National Intramural Association.

9.   National Junior College Athletic Association.

10.   Phi Epsilon Kappa (professional fraternity).

    5.2   **Identify professional literature and research in physical education.**

1.   *AAU Publication Amateur Athlete Yearbook.*

2.   *AAU News* (monthly).

3.   *American Academy of Physical Education* (position papers, studies for and by the academy).

4.   *Journal of Physical Education, Recreation and Dance.*

5.   *Research Quarterly for Exercise and Sport.*

6.   *Update.*

7.   *School Health Review.*

8.   *The Foil* - the official publication of Delta Psi Kappa (newsletter The Psi Kappa Shield).

9.   *NEA* - Today's Education.

10.   *National Jr. College Athletic Association.*

11. *Journal of Physical Education* - published bimonthly.

12. *YMCA Magazine* - Public affairs news.

5.3   Identification of effective means of promoting the physical education curriculum.

Effectively promoting the physical education curriculum **entails relating physical education to accomplishing the purposes of the entire educational process.** By providing satisfying, successful, and enriching experiences that are properly taught, physical educators shape a physically, mentally, and socially fit society. **Physical education must be related to the total educational process through the cognitive, affective, and psychomotor domains.**

Physical education in the Cognitive Domain: contributes to academic achievement, contributes to higher thought processes via motor activity, contributes to knowledge of exercise, health and disease, contributes to an understanding of the human body, contributes to an understanding of the role of physical activity and sport in the American culture, and contributes to the knowledgeable consumption of goods and services.

Physical education in the Affective Domain: contributes to self-actualization, self-esteem, and a healthy response to physical activity; contributes to an appreciation of beauty, contributes to directing one's life toward worthy goals, emphasizes humanism, affords individuals the opportunity to enjoy rich social experiences through play, assists cooperative play with others, teaches courtesy, fair play, and good sportsmanship; contributes to humanitarianism.

Physical education through the Psychomotor Domain: contributes to movement skills as a participant and spectator in sports and other physical activities; contributes skills to utilize leisure hours in mental and cultural pursuits; contributes skills necessary to the preservation of the natural environment.

Bibliography

Bucher, Charles A. *Foundations of Physical Education.* 7th ed. St. Louis: Times
     Mirror/Mosby, 1975.

Bucher, Charles A., and Deborah A. Wuest. *Foundations of Physical Education and Sport.*
     10th ed. St. Louis: Times Mirror/Mosby, 1987.

Wuest, Deborah A., and Charles A. Bucher. *Foundations of Physical Education and Sport.*
     11th ed. St. Louis: Mosby, 1991.

6.0 Knowledge of physical education supervision and management.

6.1. Identify the techniques for care and prevention of injuries in physical activities.

Strategies for preventing injuries are as follows:

1. Participant screening - evaluate injury history, anticipate and prevent potential injuries, watch for hidden injuries, reoccurrence of an injury; maintain communication.

2. Maintain hiring standards - keep current, in-service on first aid and sports medicine, sport technique, injury prevention, clinics, workshops, communication with staff and trainers. Athletes obey rules of sportsmanship, supervision, biomechanics.

3. Conditioning - year long, knowledgeable athletes, injury vs. conditioning, access to conditioning facilities and off season practice.

4. Equipment - inspections, proper fit, and proper use.

5. Facilities - maintain standards and use safe equipment.

6. Field care - emergency procedures for serious injury.

7. Rehabilitation - objective measures such as power output on an isokinetic dynamometer.

Strategies for care of physical injuries are as follows:

1. Foot - start with good footwear, foot exercises.

2. Ankle - High top, wide, tape support, strengthen plantar (calf) dorsiflexor (shin), and ankle eversion (ankle outward), isometric.

3. Shin splints - exercise that strengthens ankle dorsiflexors.

4. Achilles tendon - dorsiflexion stretching plantorflexion strengthening (heel raises)

5. Knee- sprains, best way to prevent injury to increase strength and flexibility of calf and thigh muscles.

6. Back injury - proper body mechanics.

7. Tennis elbow - lateral epicondylitis caused by bent elbow, hitting late, not stepping into the ball, heavy rackets, rackets that are strung too tight. Shoulder strains - rotator cuff muscles that rotate humerus.

8. Head and neck injuries - avoid dangerous techniques (i.e. grabbing face mask) and carefully supervise dangerous activities like the trampoline.

6.2 Identify principles used in the selection and maintenance of equipment and facilities.

Equipment Selection - based on quality and safety, goals of physical education and athletics, selection by knowledgeable personnel, continuous (what's best year of selection may not be best the following year), service and replacement considerations, successful reconditioning vs. purchasing new equipment, participants interests, age, sex, skills, limitations; trends in athletic uniforms.

Additional Guidelines for Selection of Equipment: follow purchasing policies, relate purchasing to programming, budgeting, and financing; maintenance, legal regulation, administration considerations (good working relationships at all personnel levels), best value for money spent, consult administration when equipment and supplies are needed; participants have own equipment and supplies when necessary, purchase from reputable manufacturers and distributors; follow competitive purchasing regulations, and use school forms with clearly identified brand, trademark, and catalog specifications.

Maintaining Equipment - inspect supplies and equipment upon arrival, label supplies and equipment with organization's identification; have policies for issuing and returning supplies and equipment; keep equipment in perfect operating condition, store properly, properly clean and care for equipment (including garments).

Facility Selection Considerations: bond issues for construction, availability to girls, women, minorities, and handicapped; energy costs and conservation; community involvement, convertibility (movable walls/partitions), environment must be safe, attractive, clean, comfortable, practical and adaptable to individual needs; compliance with public health codes; effective disease control.

Maintenance of Facility - custodial staff, participants, and the physical education and athletic staffs must work together to properly maintain facility. For pools. water temperature, hydrogen ion concentration, and chlorine need daily monitoring. Gymnasium play areas need to be free from dust and dirt. Showers and drying areas need daily cleaning and disinfecting. Participants' clothing should meet health standards to prevent odors and thriving germs. Turfs of outdoor playing fields must be cleared of rocks and kept free of holes and uneven surfaces; disinfect and clean drinking fountains, sinks, urinals, and toilets daily; air and sanitize lockers frequently.

6.3 Identify class management techniques to enhance the learning experience.

The first few weeks of the school year is most effective in teaching classes management structure (behavior rules, regular reminder of rules, and terms for compliance and violation of rules and routines compelling students to continue class business without disrupting the educational process).

All essential procedures and routines (roll call, excuses, tardiness, changing and showering) must be managed to productively use available class time. Good class management also insures the safety of the group through procedures and routines, provides a controlled classroom atmosphere to make instruction easier, promotes individual self-discipline and self-motivation, develops a sense of responsibility towards others and themselves within students, develops rapport between teacher and students that promotes learning, creates a group camaraderie where each student feels good within him/herself and feels at ease within the group, uses the teacher's time and energy productively; organizes and coordinates classes for the most effective instruction and learning (safety).

Long-term planning for the semester and year as well as daily, weekly, and seasonal planning is necessary. Activities need to be planned to proceed with precision and dispatched with minimal standing around time and with maximum activity time for each student. Activities need to be arranged in advance as well as any line markings.

To determine students' progress and effectiveness of teaching, measurement and evaluation should be planned. Instructors also must wear suitable clothing, have good knowledge of the subject, and be able to promote desirable attitudes and understandings toward fitness, skill learning, good sportsmanship, and other physical education objectives should be consistently emphasized.

Bibliography

Arnheim, Daniel. *Modern Principles of Athletic Training.* 7th ed. St. Louis: Times Mirror/Mosby, 1989.

Bucher, Charles A. *Management of Physical Education and Athletic Training Programs.* 7th ed. St. Louis: Times Mirror/Mosby, 1987.

Bucher, Charles A., and Constance R. Koenig. *Methods and Materials for Secondary School Physical Education.* 6th ed. St. Louis: The C.V. Mosby Company, 1983.

Fahey, Thomas. *Athletic Training.* Palo Alto, CA: Mayfield, 1986.

Harrison, Joyce. *Instructional Strategies for Physical Education.* Dubuque, IA: Brown, 1983.

Horine, Larry. *Administration of Physical Education and Sports Programs.* Philadelphia: Saunders College Publishing, 1985.

Jensen, Clayne R. (1983). *Administrative Management of Physical Education and Athletic Programs.* Philadelphia: Lea & Febiger.

Keller, Irvin A., and Charles. E. Forsythe. *Administration of High School Athletics.* 7th ed. Englewood Cliffs, NJ: Prentice-Hall, 1984.

Mood, Dale, Frank F. Musker, and Judith E. Rink. *Sports and Recreational Activities.* 9th ed. St. Louis: Times Mirror/Mosby, 1987.

Siedentop, Daryl. *Physical Education: Teaching and Curriculum Strategies for Grades 5-12.* Palo Alto, CA: Mayfield, 1986.

7.0   Knowledge of legal aspects in teaching physical education.

7.1.   Identify major state and federal <u>legislative</u> enactment's to the physical education curricula.

<u>Graduation Requirements.</u>

Education reforms enacted by the 1983 Florida legislature included for the first time in Florida's history statewide minimum high school graduation requirements.

Beginning with the 86/87 school year, successful completion of a minimum of 24 credits in grades nine through twelve shall be required for graduation. Fifteen of the 24 credits are specified in law.

Included in the specified 15 credits are the following physical education, dance, and health requirements:

1. Half credit in physical education.

2. Half credit in performing fine arts to be selected from music, dance, drama, or art form that requires manual dexterity.

3. Half credit in life management skills to include consumer education, positive emotional development, nutrition, information and instruction on breast cancer detection and breast self-examination, cardiopulmonary resuscitation, drug education, and hazards of smoking.

Schools are encouraged to exceed established requirements for high school graduation. School districts do vary in physical education requirements. Some require two credits, some one and a half, some one credit and some state the minimum half credit.

<u>Establishment of curriculum frameworks and student performance standards.</u>

A curriculum framework is defined in law as a set of broad guidelines which aid educational personnel in producing specific instructional plans for a given subject or study area. The legislative intent was to promote a degree of <u>uniformity and instructional consistency</u> in curriculum offerings.

Student achievement is related to the intended outcomes of the selected curriculum frameworks. Student performance standards for 40 physical education courses and 15 dance courses were developed.

Students usually take the Personal Fitness course in either the ninth or tenth grade. Recommended implementation strategies include three days of laboratory activity and two days of classroom instruction per week.

<u>Federal Legislation:</u>

The Department of Health and Human Services recommended legislative changes - including those for education. **Title IX prohibits sex discrimination in educational programs and PL 94-142 requires schools to provide educational services for handicapped students.**

State Legislation:

Primarily, state governments (Department of Education), are responsible for education. Departments of education establish policies for course curriculum, number of class days and class time, and amount of credits to be earned to graduate.

Impact of education reforms:

Enrollment went up and there was a renewed administrative, parental, and student support. Additional impacts include: coeducational classes, separate teams for boys and girls and men and women must be secured otherwise a coeducational team must be created, equal opportunities for both sexes must be provided (for facilities, equipment and supplies, practice and game, medical and training services, academic tutoring and coaching, travel and per diem allowances, and dining and housing facilities), equitable expenditure of funds for both sexes.

All state and local laws and conference regulations that conflict with Title IX are overruled, and federal aid (even when not related to Physical Education or athletics) must be in compliance with Title IX. There is no discrimination for personnel standards and scholarships must be awarded equitably.

7.2   Recognize the areas of <u>legal liability</u> applicable to physical education.

1. Tort - A legal wrong resulting in a direct or indirect injury, can be an omission. Act intended or unintended to cause harm.

2. Negligence - someone not fulfilling the legal duty according to common reasoning.

3. In loco parentis - acting in the place of the parent in relation to the child.

4. Negligence concerning equipment and facilities.

5. Negligence concerning instruction.

6. Negligence in athletic participation. One must consider sex, size and skill of each participant.

7. Sports Product Liability - liability of the manufacturer to the person using the manufacturer's product who sustains injury/damage from utilizing the product.

8. Violence and legal liability (intentional injury in sports contests) - harmful, unpermitted contact of one person by another (referred to as battery).

9. Physical education classes held off campus and legal liability - primary concern is providing due care which is the responsibility of management and staff members of sponsoring organization. Failing to observe "due care" can result in negligence.

The immunity derived from the old common-law rule that a government agency cannot be sued without its consent is slowly changing in the eyes of the court so that now both state and federal governments may be sued.

Those elements of the school curriculum that are compulsory, such as physical education, prompt courts to decide on the basis of what is in the best interests of the public.

Although school districts have been granted immunity in many states, teachers do not have such immunity. Whether employed by private person or a municipal corporation every employee owes a duty not to injure another by a negligent act of commission.

7.3. Recognize actions that promote safety and reduce possibilities of litigation.

Actions that can avoid lawsuits include the following:

1. Knowing the health status of each person in the program.

2. Considering the ability and skill level when selecting new activities.

3. Grouping with equal competitive levels.

4. Using safe equipment and facilities.

5. Organizing and supervising classes.

6. Never leaving a class.

7. Knowing first aid (Do not diagnose or prescribe).

8. Keeping accident records.

9. Giving instruction prior to dangerous activities.

10. Being sure that injured students get medical attention and examination.

11. Getting exculpatory agreements (parental consent forms).

12. Having a planned, written disposition for students who become ill or are injured.

13. Providing a detailed accident report if one occurs.

Actions that promote safety include the following:

1. Having an instructor who is properly trained and qualified.

2. Organizing the class by size, activity, and conditions of the class.

3. Inspecting the mats.

4. Avoiding overcrowding.

5. Using adequate lighting.

6. Ensuring that children are dressed in appropriate sneakers that are worn on the gymnasium floor.

7. Presenting organized activities.

8. Inspecting all equipment regularly.

9. Adhering to building codes and fire regulations.

10. Using protective equipment.

11. Using spotters.

12. Eliminating hazards.

13. Teaching participants correct ways of performing skills/activities and the use of equipment.

14. Inspecting buildings and other facilities regularly and immediately giving notice of any hazards.

Bibliography

Bucher, Charles A. *Management of Physical Education and Athletic Training Programs.* 9th ed. St. Louis: Times Mirror/Mosby, 1987.

Bucher, Charles A., and Constance R. Koenig. *Methods and Materials for Secondary School Physical Education.* 6th ed. St. Louis: The C.V. Mosby Company, 1983.

Harrison, Joyce M. *Instructional Strategies for Physical Education.* Dubuque, IA: Brown, 1983.

Harageones, Manny. " The Quality of Florida High School Physical Education Programs." *Journal of Physical Education* 58 (1987): 52-54.

Horine, Larry. *Administration of Physical Education and Sports Programs.* Philadelphia: Saunders College Publishing, 1985.

Jensen, Clayne. R. *Administrative Management of Physical Education and Athletic Programs.* Philadelphia: Lea & Febiger.

8.0   Knowledge of factors affecting the learning environment.

    8.1   Identify modifications of the learning environment which <u>enhance participation in physical education.</u>

There are three options for maximizing participation: activity modification, multi-activity designs, and homogeneous or heterogeneous grouping.

Activity modification is the first option to employ to achieve maximum calculated participation by simply modifying the type of equipment used or the rules that apply. However, keep activity as close to original as possible (i.e. substitute a yarn ball for a birdie for badminton).

Multi-activity designs permit greater diversification of equipment and more efficient use of available facilities (keeps all students involved).

Homogeneous and heterogeneous grouping for the purpose of individualized instruction, enhancing self-concepts, equalizing competition, and promoting cooperation among classmates.

Furthermore, plan activities that encourage the greatest amount of participation by utilizing all available facilities and equipment, involve students in planning class work/activities, and be flexible. Tangible rewards and praise can also be used.

    8.2   Identify appropriate activities and adaptation for students with limitations.

Appropriate activities are those activities and environments that handicapped students can be placed in where they can successfully participate.

Adaptations include: individualized instruction and modifying rules, modifying environments, and modifying tasks. As needs warrant, participants can be moved to less restrictive environments (including periodic assessments of person to advance his/her placement and review progress and to determine what least restrictive environment means to the participant including changing services to produce future optimum progress). However, the most appropriate placement depends on meeting the physical education needs of the handicapped person, and the environment should promote social interaction.

Functional Adaptations Include:

Blind participants can receive auditory or tactual clues to help them find objects or to position their bodies in the activity area. Blind students also can learn the patterns of movement by manually motioning them the correct pattern by verbal instructions.

Deaf students can read lips or learn signing to communicate and understand instructions.

Physically challenged students may have to use crutches to enable them to move.

Asthmatics can play goalie or similar positions requiring less cardiorespiratory demands for activities.

Simplifying rules can accommodate a retarded participant's limited comprehension.

Adapting Selected Activities:

Walking: adapt distance, distance over time, number of steps in specified distance, hand rails for support, change slope for incline walking, and change width of walking pathway.

Stairclimbing: change pathway, pace of climbing, and number and height of steps.

Running: change utilizing distance over time, using an incline changing slope (distance over time), and for a maze (distance over time).

Jumping: change distance and height of jump, change distance in a series and from a platform, change participants arm positions.

Hopping: change distance for one and two hops (using preferred and nonpreferred leg) and distance through obstacle course.

Galloping: change number of gallops over distance, change distance covered in number of gallops, and widen pathway.

Skipping: change number of errorless skips, change distance covered in number of skips, change number of skips in distance, and add music for skipping in rhythm.

Leaping: change distance and height of leaps.

Bouncing balls: change size of ball (larger), have participant use two hands, reduce number of dribbles, bounce ball higher, have participant stand stationary and perform bounces one at a time.

Catching: use larger balls and have participant catch balls that are thrown chest high from a lower height of release, shorten catching distance, have participant stop and then catch ball (easier than moving and catching).

Adapting for Problems of Strength, Endurance, and Power Activities:

1. Lower basketball goal or nets; increase size of target.

2. Decrease throwing distance between partners, serving distance and wazzu net, and distance between bases.

3. Reduce size or weight of projectiles or balls to be thrown.

4. Shorten length and/or reduce weight of bat or other striking apparatus.

5. Play games in lying or sitting positions to lower center of gravity.

6. Select a "slow ball" (it will not get away too fast) or deflate ball in case it has to be chased or attach a string to the ball for recovery.

7. Reduce playing time and lower number of points to win.

8. Use more frequent rest periods.

9. Rotate often or use frequent substitution when needed.

10. Use mobilization alternatives such as using scooter boards one inning/period and then one inning/period on feet.

Adapting for Balance and Agility Problems:

1. Verify if balance problem is due to medication (may have to consult physician).

2. Use chairs, tables, or barre to help with stability.

3. Have participants learn to optimally utilize eyes for balance skills.

4. Teach various ways to fall and incorporate dramatics into fall activities.

5. Use carpeted surfaces.

6. Lower center of gravity.

7. Have participant extend arms or provide a lightweight pole.

8. Have participant keep as much of his/her body in contact with the surface.

9. Widen base of support (distance between feet).

10. Increase width of walking parameters.

Adapting for Coordination and Accuracy:

Throwing Activities: use beanbags, yarn or nerf balls, and/or smaller sized balls.

Catching and Striking Activities: use larger, softer, and lighter balls, throw balls to mid-line, shorten distance, and reduce speed of balls.

Striking Kicking Activities: enlarge striking surface, choke up on bats, begin with participant successfully striking stationary objects then progress to striking with movement, and increase target size/goal cage.

Exercise Physiology Adaptations: decrease the amount of resistive weight, amount of reps and sets, pace and/or distance of exercise, intensity, and increase the amount of intervals and combine together any of previous modifications.

Bibliography

Auxter, David, and Jean Pyfer. *Principles and Methods of Adapted Physical Education and Recreation.* 5th ed. St. Louis: Times Mirror/Mosby, 1985.

Bucher, Charles A., and Constance R. Koenig. *Methods and Materials for Secondary School Physical Education.* 6th ed. St. Louis: The C.V. Mosby Company, 1983.

9.0 Knowledge of Physical Education <u>evaluation techniques</u>.

    9.1 Use <u>skill assessment</u> in the evaluation of student performance.

        A. General Skills:

          1. <u>Iowa Brace Test</u> for motor educability.

          2. <u>AAHPERD Youth Fitness Test</u> for motor capacity.

          3. <u>AAHPERD Health Related Physical Fitness Test</u> for physical capacity.

          4. <u>McCloy's General Motor Ability and Capacity Test</u> for motor ability and motor efficiency.

          5. <u>Rodgers Strength Test</u>.

          6. <u>Texas PE Test</u> measures motor ability.

          7. Skills test for accuracy involve kicking, throwing or striking an object toward a goal that can be performed by volleyballs serves, basketball free throws, badminton short serves, basketball passing (i.e. AAHPERD Basketball Passing Test for Accuracy).

          8. <u>Skills test for total bodily movement</u> requires performing a test course with movements similar to the sport (i.e. AAHPERD Basketball Control Test).

          9. <u>Wall Volley Tests</u> measures number of consecutive successful time/trials to pass, kick, throw, or strike an object at a wall in a given time (i.e. AAHPERD Basketball Passing Test).

         10. <u>Skills Tests for Power or Distance</u> involve kicks, throws, or strokes to measure the ability to forcibly kick, throw, or strike an object (i.e. Badminton Drive for Distance; Cornish Handball Power Test).

         11. <u>Combination Tests</u> are composed of previous groupings to assess speed and accuracy.

        B. Teacher Ratings - create a numerical scale from one to five. Rank performance based on specific observable movements. An example would be in a creative movement class. Evaluate the use of space, use of focus, variety of movements.

        C. Student Progress - score improvements (i.e. Archery, badminton); charting (basketball shots missed).

Skills tests for specific sports can be administered in one of two ways: (1) by rating individual performance based on a specified number of trials, or (2) by evaluating skills using norm referenced scales for a specific grade level.

Problems with skill tests are that they take too much time to administer and secondly, the reliability may not be valid.

To measure affective domain the teacher can observe the student and keep a record of those observations. A second way to measure affect is to use opinion polls. A third way to measure affect is to use rating scales.

To measure the social progress of an individual use a sociogram. It plots the associations an individual student has with his peers.

9.2   Identify Methods of Evaluation in the Affective Domain.

(includes interests, appreciations, attitudes, values, & adjustments inherent in the acquisition of physical activities)

1. Social Measures (behavior, leadership, acceptance, and personality/character):

- Harrocks Prosocial Behavior Inventory (HPBBI) - measures prosocial play behavior of 5th and 6th graders in recreational play.

- Adams Prosocial Inventory - measures high school students prosocial behaviors in physical education classes.

- Nelson Leadership Questionnaire - determines leaders as perceived by instructors, coaches, classmates, and teammates.

- Cowell Personal Distance Scale - measures congruity of a student within a group and his/her yearly development.

- Blanchard Behavior Rating Scale - measures students' personality and character.

2. Attitudes Measures (predispositions to actions):

- McKethan Student Attitude Inventory-Instructional Processes in Secondary Physical Education (SAI-IPSPE) - measures attitudes of students' for instructional processes (teacher's verbal behavior, nature of activities, patterns of class organization, and regulations and policies in concept physical education environment).

- Toulmin Elementary Physical Education Attitude Scale (TEPEAS) - measures attitudes of the physical education program of elementary school students.

- Feelings About Physical Activity - measures commitment to activity

- Children's Attitudes Toward Physical Activity - Revised (CATPA) - measures significance students have toward physical activity.

- Willis Sports Attitudes Inventory - Form C : measures motives of competition in sports (achievement, power, success; avoiding failure).

- Sport Orientation Questionnaire Form B: measures behaviors of achievement and competition during exercising and sports.

- McMahan Sportsmanship Questionnaire - measures high school students attitudes of sportsmanship.

- Physical Estimation and Attraction Scale - measures motivation and interest.

3. **Self-Concept Measures** (self-perception):

- Cratly Adaptation of Piers-Harris Self-Concept and Scale - measures/estimates students' own feelings about their appearance and skill performance abilities.

- Merkley Measure of Actual Physical Self - measures perception of physical self relating to exercise and activity.

- Nelson-Allen Movement Satisfaction - measures satisfaction of movement.

- Tanner Movement Satisfaction Scale - measures students' own level of satisfaction/dissatisfaction with their own movement.

4. **Stress and Anxiety:**

- Stress Inventory (Miller and Allen) - measures level of stress according to stress indicators.

- Sport Competition Anxiety Tests - measures anxiety toward competition via one's perception of the competition as threatening events.

9.3   Identify Methods of Evaluation in the Cognitive Domain of Learning.

1. Standardized Tests - scientifically constructed test with validity and reliability established.

2. Teacher-made Tests - developed by the teacher him/herself.

3. Essay Tests - organizing information presented, logically, in written paragraphs.

4. Objective Tests - true/false, multiple choice, matching, diagrams, completion, or short written response.

5. Norm-Referenced Tests - compares individual's score to the scores of others.

6. Criterion-Referenced Tests - interpreting a score by comparing it to a predetermined standard.

Bibliography

Barrow, Harold M., Rosemary McGee, and Kathleen A. Tritschler. *Practical Measurement in Physical Education and Sport.* 4th ed. Philadelphia: Lea & Febiger.

Baumgartner, Ted A., and Andrew S. Jackson. *Measurement for Evaluation in Physical Education.* Boston: Houghton Mifflin Co., 1975.

Baumgartner, Ted A., and Andrew S. Jackson. *Measurement for Evaluation in Physical Education and Exercise Science.* 3rd ed. Dubuque, IA: Wm. C. Brown Publishers, 1987.

Clarke, H. Harrison, and David H. Clarke. *Application of Measurement to Physical Education.* 6th ed. Englewood Cliffs, NJ: Prentice-Hall, 1987.

Kirkendall, Don R., Joseph J. Gruber, and Robert E. Johnson. *Measurement and Evaluation for Physical Educators.* 2nd ed. Champaign, IL: Human Kinetics, 1987.

Safrit, Margret J, and Terry M. Wood. *Introduction to Measurement in Physical Education and Exercise Science.* 3rd ed. St. Louis: Times Mirror/Mosby, 1995.

10.0 Knowledge of body management components

10.1 Identify and define locomotor skills.

Locomotor skills move an individual from one point to another.

1. Walking - with one foot contacting the surface at all times, walking shifts one's weight from one foot to the other while legs swing alternately in front of the body.

2. Running - an extension of walking that has a phase where the body is propelled with no base of support (speed is faster, stride is longer, and arms add power).

3. Jumping - projectile movements that momentarily suspend the body in midair.

4. Vaulting - coordinated movements that allow oneself to spring over an obstacle.

5. Leaping - similar to running but leaping has greater height, flight, and distance.

6. Hopping - using the same foot to take off from a surface and land.

7. Galloping - forward or backward advanced elongation of walking that is combined and coordinated with a leap.

8. Sliding - sideward stepping pattern that can be uneven, long or short.

9. Body Rolling - moving across a surface by rocking back and forth, by turning over and over or by shaping the body into a revolving mass.

10. Climbing - ascending or descending using the hands and feet with the upper body using the most control.

10.2 Identify and define nonlocomotor skills.

Nonlocomotor skills are stability skills where there is movement with little or no movement of one's base of support.

1. Bending - movement around a joint where two body parts meet.

2. Dodging - sharp change of direction from original line of movement such as away from a person or object.

3. Stretching - extending/hyperextending joints to make body parts as straight or as long as possible.

4. Twisting - rotating body/body parts around an axis with a stationary base.

5. Turning - circular moving the body through space releasing the base of support.

6. Swinging - circular/pendular movements of the body/body parts below an axis.

7. Swaying - same as swinging but movement is above an axis.

8. Pushing - applying force against an object or person to move it away from one's body or to move one's body away from the object or person.

9. Pulling - executing force to cause objects/people to move toward one's body.

10.3   Identify and define manipulative skills.

(Using body parts to propel or receive an object; controlling objects primarily with the hands and feet. Two types: receptive = catch + trap; propulsive = throw, strike; kick).

1. <u>Bouncing/Dribbling</u> - projecting a ball downwards.

2. <u>Catching</u> - stopping momentum of an object (for control) using the hands.

3. <u>Kicking</u> - striking an object with the foot.

4. <u>Rolling</u> - initiating force to an object to instill contact with a surface.

5. <u>Striking</u> - giving impetus to an object with the use of the hands or an object.

6. <u>Throwing</u> - using one or both arms to project an object into midair away from the body.

7. <u>Trapping</u> - without the use of the hands, receiving and controlling a ball.

Bibliography:

Gabbard, Carl, Elizabeth LeBlanc, and Susan Lowry. *Physical Education for Children: Building the Foundation.* 2nd ed. Englewood Cliffs, NJ: Prentice-Hall, 1994.

Gallahue, David L. *Understanding Motor Development in Children.* New York: John Wiley & Sons, 1982.

Gallahue, David L. *Developmental Physical Education for Today's Children.* 2nd ed. Dubuque, IA: Wm. C. Brown, 1993.

Nicols, Beverly. *Moving and Learning: The Elementary School Physical Education Experience.* 3rd ed. St. Louis: Mosby-Year Book, 1994.

Pica, Rae. *Experiences in Movement.* Albany, NY: Delmar Publishing Inc., 1995.

Wuest, Deborah A., and Charles A. Bucher. *Foundations of Physical Education and Sport.* 11th ed. St. Louis: Mosby, 1991.

11.0   Knowledge of movement concepts.

11. 1   Apply concept of body awareness to physical education activities.

Body awareness is one's impression of own body parts and their, the body parts, capability of movement.

Body awareness can be assessed by playing and watching a game of "Simon Says" and asking the students to touch different body parts. Children can also be instructed to make their bodies into various shapes from straight to round to twisted varying sizes to fit into different sized spaces.

In addition, children can be instructed to touch one part of the body to another and to use various body parts to do something. For instance, children can be told to stomp their feet, twist their neck, clap their hands, nod their heads, wiggle their noses, wiggle their toes, snap their fingers, open their mouths, shrug their shoulders, bend their knees, bend their elbows, and close their eyes.

11.2   Apply the concept of spatial awareness to physical education activities.

Spatial awareness - making decisions of an object's positional changes in space (awareness of three dimensional space position changes).

Developing spatial awareness requires two sequential phases: 1) the location of objects in relation to one's own body in space, and 2) locating more than one object in relation to each object and independent of one's own body.

Plan activities using different size balls or using boxes or hoops and have children move: near and away, under and over, in front and behind, and inside and outside and beside the objects.

11.3   Apply the concept of effort qualities to physical education.
(Qualities of movement applying the mechanical principles of balance, time, and force).

- Balance - activities for balance include having children move on their hands and feet, leaning, movements on lines, and balancing and holding shapes while they are moving.

- Time - activities using the concept of time can involve having students move as fast as they can and as slow as they can in specified movement patterns that are timed.

- Force - activities using the concept of force can include having students use their bodies to produce enough force to move them through space. They can also paddle balls against walls, and jump over objects with various heights.

Bibliography

Gabbard, Carl, Elizabeth LeBlanc, and Susan Lowry. *Physical Education for Children: Building the Foundation.* 2nd ed. Englewood Cliffs, NJ: Prentice-Hall.

Gallahue, David L. *Understanding Motor Development in Children.* New York: John Wiley & Sons, 1982.

Gallahue, David L. *Developmental Physical Education for Today's Children.* 2nd ed. Dubuque, IA: Wm. C. Brown, 1993.

Hoffman, Hubert A., Jane Young, and Stephen Klesius. *Meaningful Movement for Children.* Boston: Allyn and Bacon, Inc., 1981.

Nicols, Beverly. *Moving and Learning: The Elementary School Physical Education Experience.* 3rd ed. St. Louis: Mosby-Year Book, 1994.

Wuest, Deborah A., and Charles A. Bucher. *Foundations of Physical Education and Sport.* 11th ed. St. Louis: Mosby.

12.0 Knowledge of mechanical principles of body management.

12.1 Apply the concept of equilibrium to movement.

When body segments are moved independently, body mass is redistributed which changes the location of the body's center of gravity. Segments also move to change the body's base of support from one moment to the next to cope with imminent loss of balance.

The entire center of gravity of the body shifts in the same direction of movement of the body's segments. As long as the center of gravity is located over the base of support, the body will remain in a state of equilibrium. And, the more the center of gravity is situated over the base, the greater the stability. Stability is enhanced when the base of support is increased and/or the center of gravity is lowered. To be effective, the base of support needs to be widened in the direction of force produced or opposed by the body. Shifting weight in the direction of the force in conjunction with widening the base of support further enhances stability.

Dynamic balance is accomplished by the constant interaction of forces that move the body in the elected direction and speed by a smooth transition of the center of gravity changing from one base of support to the next.

12.2 Apply the concept of force to movement. (Any influence that can change the state of motion of an object; objective of movement must be considered).

- Magnitude of Force - inertia of the object and any other resisting forces must be overcome by enough force for movement to occur, and the force must have adequate magnitude to overcome inertia.

For linear movement, the closer the force is applied to the center of gravity, the less force is needed to move an object.

For rotational movement, the farther the force is applied to the center of gravity, the less force is required to rotate an object.

For objects with a fixed point - unless force is applied through the point of fixation, the object will rotate.

- Energy - capacity to do work. (The more energy a body has, the greater the force with which it can move something [or change its shape] and/or the farther it can move it.

Movement (mechanical energy) has two types:

1. Potential energy (energy possessed by virtue of position, absolute location in space or change in shape.

   A. *Gravitational potential energy* - potential energy of an object that is in a position from which it can fall or be lowered gravity.

   B. *Elastic (strain) potential energy* - energy potential of an object to do work while recoiling (or reforming) after it has been stretched, compressed, or twisted.

2. Kinetic energy (energy possessed by virtue of motion and increases with speed).

<u>Force Absorption</u> - maintaining equilibrium while receiving a moving object's kinetic energy without sustaining injury or without losing balance while rebounding. The force of impact is dependent on an object's weight and speed. The more abrupt kinetic energy is lost, the more likely injury or rebound occurs. Thus, *absorbing force requires gradually decelerating a moving mass by utilization of smaller forces over a longer period of time.* Stability is greater when the force is received closer to the center of gravity.

Striking resistive surfaces - the force of impact per unit area decreases when the moving object's area of surface making contact is increased and the surface of the area that the object strikes is increased.

Striking non-resistive surfaces - the force of impact is reduced if the moving object's area of surface making contact is decreased because it is more likely to penetrate.

The more time and distance that motion is stopped for a moving object to strike any surface, the more gradual the force of impact is absorbed, and the reaction forces acting upon the moving object are diminished.

Equilibrium is regained easily when the moving body (striking a resistive surface) more vertically aligns the center of gravity over the base of support.

Angular force against a body can be reduced by making contact of a moving object closer to the body and making contact closer to the center of gravity. Also, widening the base of support in the direction of the moving object increases stability.

12.3   Apply concept of leverage to movement.

Muscle force is applied where muscles insert on bones.

1. <u>First class lever</u> - the axis is located between the points of application of the force and of the resistance.

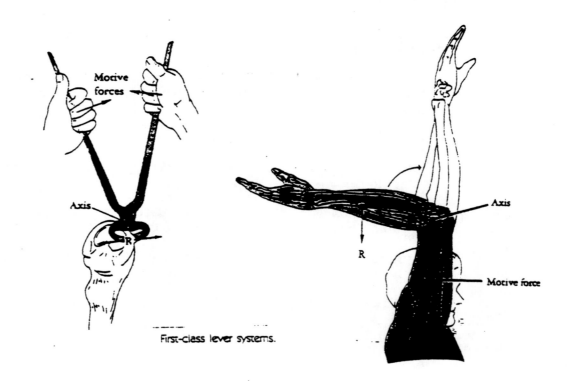

First-class lever systems.

2. <u>Second class lever</u> - the force arm is longer than the resistance arm (resistance is applied between the axis and the point of application of the force).

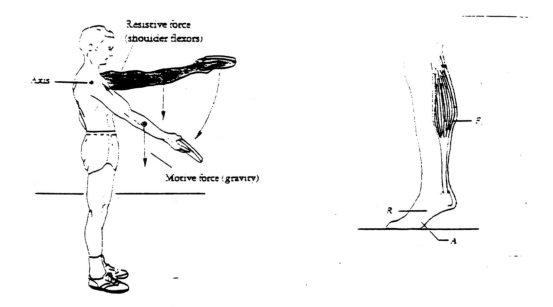

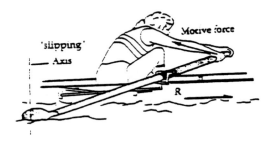

Second-class lever systems.

3. <u>Third class lever</u> - the force works at a point between the axis and the resistance (resistance arm is always longer than the force arm).

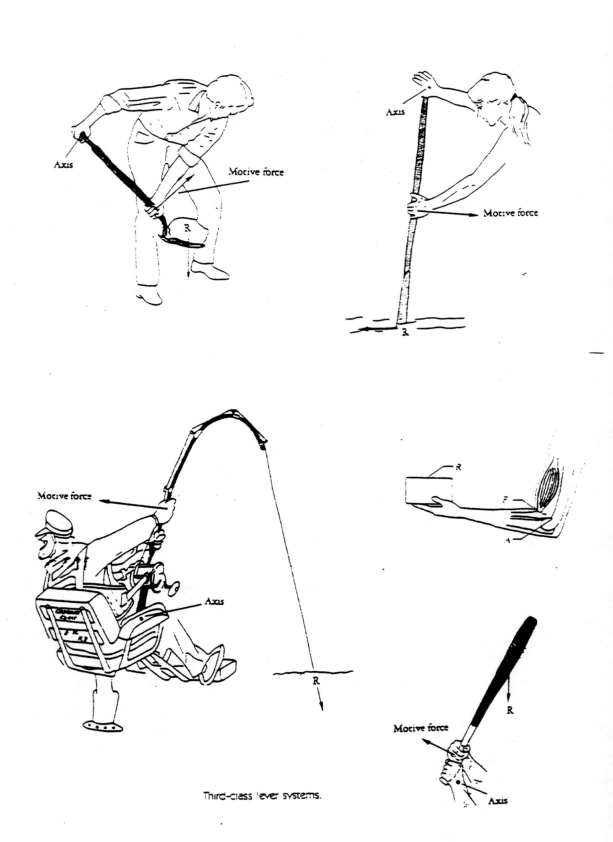

Third-class lever systems.

With a few exceptions, the body is basically assembled with third class levers with bones functioning as the levers, and the fulcrum supplied by innervated muscles contracting or by gravity acting on various body masses. As a result, the human body favors speed and range of motion over force.

Because most human body levers are long, their distal ends are capable of moving rapidly. Thus, the body is capable of swift, wide movements at the expense of abundant muscle force.

Tasks involving rapid movement with light objects are easily performed by the human body. Very heavy tasks require a device for the body to secure an advantage of force.

Sports instruments increase body levers, thereby, increasing the speed of an object's imparting force. However, more muscle force is required to use sports instruments.

The body's leverage, rarely, includes one part of the body (a simple, singular lever). Movement of the body is an outcome of a system of levers that operate together. However, levers do function in sequence when the force produced by the system of levers is dependent on the speed at the extremity. Many levers function simultaneously for a heavy task (i.e. Pushing).

12.4 Apply mechanical principles of motion to physical education activities.

1. **Inertia** - tendency of a body or object to remain in its present state of motion; an object will stay in a prescribed straight path and will move at its given speed unless some force acts to change it.

- *Projecting objects for vertical distance* - the forces of gravity and air resistance prevent an object that is projected vertically to continue at its given velocity. The downward, resistive force of gravity slows a projectile directed upward until it halts (at the peak of vertical path). At this point, the downward force of gravity becomes an incentive force that increases the speed of the object until it confronts another force (the earth or other external object) that slows the object until it stops. When the object no longer is ascending and begins to descend, gravity alters the object's direction of motion.

Air resistance (of still air) always opposes the object's motion. Therefore, an ascending object's air resistance is downward, and a descending object's air resistance is upward. An increase in velocity increases air-drag force that decreases the magnitude of the drag as the object continuously moves upward slowing in velocity, and the magnitude of the drag increases as the object moves faster and faster downward. Moreover, the direction and magnitude of the object's acceleration, due to the force of gravity, are constant while direction and magnitude of changes, due to air resistance, are dependent on the object's speed and direction.

To a projectile's maximum height it will travel after being released, the longer an object moves upward, the farther upward it travels until the resistive forces of gravity and air resistance slow it to zero vertical velocity. Thus, an object travels the highest when projected with the greatest velocity, and neither gravity's upward deceleration nor its downward acceleration are affected by the object's weight. But, the object's weight is a factor to calculate in its net force acting on the object's vertical movement through the air.

- *Projecting the body for vertical distance* - for these activities, the height of reach of the hand from the ground is the significant factor. The following three factors determine the body's reach height: 1) the center of gravity's vertical velocity, 2) the center of gravity's height from the ground at takeoff, and 3) the vertical distance of the fingertips relative to the center of gravity at the peak of the jump.

- *Projecting for vertical distance with a horizontal component* - for these activities, a running approach to the point of takeoff produces some horizontal velocity even with a 100% vertical takeoff.

- *Projecting for horizontal distance* - a body will continue to travel horizontally until it is halted by an external force, usually the ground. Gravity stops vertical movement while ground friction eventually stops horizontal velocity preventing any additional horizontal distance. "Air time" is increased when the initial upward vertical velocity component is greater. There must be a tradeoff between maximum "air time" (determined by vertical velocity) and maximum horizontal distance (determined by horizontal velocity).

- *Horizontal projections where takeoff and landing heights are equal* - maximum horizontal distance is accomplished with a 45 degree projection angle.

- *Horizontal projections where takeoff and landing heights are uneven* - an object's height of center of gravity is dependent on a performer's height and his/her location, in relation to the ground, upon release or impact of the object. An object's greater travel time forward (via extra vertical distance), the farther the object's distance before landing. Hence, a performer who is taller has an automatic advantage over a shorter performer who throws with the same projection velocity. And, the greater the difference between takeoff and landing heights, the smaller the optimum angle of release - given equal projection velocities.

Projecting objects for accuracy:

- Vertical plane targets - accuracy is easiest when using a trajectory that is perpendicular to the target as it coincides with the target face. As projection distance increases, a more curved parabolic path is required.

- Horizontal plane targets - the more vertically the projectile arrives at the target (as close to 90 degrees as possible), the more likelihood of successfully hitting the target and minimizing the object from rolling or sliding away from the target area.

Projecting the body for accuracy - for moving or positioning the body (or its segments) to achieve an ideal/model performance by body maneuvers, the body's center of gravity is projected to an imaginary target point in space.

Projecting objects for accuracy when speed may enhance the performance - the angle must be increased for slower projection speeds (must consider participant's height).

2. **Acceleration** - the movement response (acceleration) of a system depends not only on how much net external force is applied to it but also on the resistance to movement change (inertia).

If an object's acceleration is proportional to the applied force, then the greater the force applied, the greater the acceleration. An object's acceleration is inversely proportional to its mass (the greater the mass, the less the acceleration).

- *Angular acceleration* (rate that an object's angular speed or direction is changed) - angular acceleration will be great if there is a large change in angular velocity in a short amount of time. A rigid body (or segment) encounters angular acceleration or deceleration only when a net external torque is applied. When torque stops, a new velocity is reached and maintained until another torque is applied. Acceleration is always in the direction of the acting torque. And, the more torque, the more the angular acceleration.

- *Linear acceleration* (time rate of change in velocity) - an object's magnitude of acceleration is significant if there is a large change of velocity in a small amount of time. When the same velocity changes over a longer period of time, acceleration is small. Acceleration is experienced only when force is applied. When the force stops, a new speed is reached by the object/body, and the object/body continues at the new speed until that speed or direction is altered by another force. In addition, the direction of acceleration is the same direction as the applied net force. To produce a vast acceleration, a large force is required. A small force produces a modest acceleration.

- *Zero/Constant Acceleration* (constant velocity) - there is no change in a system's velocity when the object/body moves at a given velocity and encounters equal, opposing forces. Hence, velocity is constant since no force causes acceleration or deceleration.

- *Acceleration caused by gravity* - a falling object/body continues to accelerate at the rate of 9.8 m/sec. (32 ft/sec.) each second it falls.

- *Radial acceleration (direction change caused by centripetal force)* - centripetal force is aimed along an illusory line (the circular path) any instant. Therefore, it is the force responsible for change of direction. The bigger the mass, the greater the centripetal force required. Direction change (radial acceleration) is also magnified with a tighter turn, so friction needs to be enhanced. Speed is constrained by maximum friction (centrifugal force). A combination of the variables mass, radius of curvature, speed of travel, and centripetal force cause radial acceleration.

3. **Action/Reaction** - every action has an equal and opposite reaction.

- *Linear motion* - the larger the mass, the more it resists motion change produced by a force.

The movement of the human body is caused by some body segment(s) exerting force in contact with a surface and the reaction from the surface moves the body. A runner is propelled forward with an equal and opposite force pushed backward against the ground (as long as the surface has sufficient friction and resistance to slipping). A canoe paddle or swimmer exerts a backward force by pushing the water backwards causing a specific velocity that is dependent on the stroke's force as well as the equal and opposite force made by the water pushing forward against the canoe paddle or arm moving the canoe or the swimmer forward.

Every torque (angular motion) exerted by one body/object on another has another torque equal in magnitude and opposite direction exerted by the second body/object on the first. Changing angular momentum must be caused by a force that is equal and opposite to change in momentum.

When action/reaction is not desired, it must be controlled by substituting and absorbing the undesired action.

Performing actions in a standing position requires the counterpressure of the ground against the feet for accurate movement of one or more parts of the body.

Bibliography

Adams, William C. *Foundations of Physical Education, Exercise, and Sport Sciences.* Philadelphia: Lea & Febiger, 1991.

Broer, Marion R., and Zernicke, Ronald F. *Efficiency of Human Movement.* 4th ed. Philadelphia: W. B. Saunders Company, 1979.

Kreighbaum, Ellen, and Katherine M. Barthels. *Biomechanics: A Qualitative Approach for Studying Human Movement.* 3rd ed. New York: Macmillan Publishing Company.

Luttgens, Kathryn, and Katherine F. Wells. *Kinesiology: Scientific Basis of Human Motion.* Philadelphia: Lea & Febiger, 1982.

Northrip, John W, Gene A. Logan, and Wayne C. McKinney. *Introduction to Biomechanical Analysis of Sport.* 2nd ed. Dubuque, IA: Wm. C. Brown.

Wuest, Deborah A. and Charles A. Bucher. *Foundations of Physical Education and Sport.* 11th ed. St. Louis: Mosby.

13.0 **Knowledge of activities for body management skill development.**

13.1 **Identify sequential development and activities for locomotor skills acquisition.**

Sequential Development = crawl, creep, walk, run, jump, hop, gallop, slide, leap, skip; step-hop.

- *Activities to develop walking skills* include walking slower and faster in place; walking forward, backward, and sideways with slower and faster paces in straight, curving, and zigzag pathways with various length of steps, pausing between steps, and changing the height of the body.

- *Activities to develop running skills* are having students pretend they are playing basketball, trying to score a touchdown, trying to catch a bus, finishing a lengthy race, and pretending they are running on a hot surface.

- *Activities to develop jumping skills* include alternating jumping with feet together and feet apart, taking off and landing on the balls of the feet, clicking the heels together while airborne, and landing with a foot forward and a foot backward.

- *Activities to develop galloping skills* include having students play a game of Fox and Hound with the lead foot being the fox and the back foot being the hound that is attempting to catch the fox (lead foot is alternated).

- *Activities to develop sliding skills* include having students hold hands in a circle and sliding in one direction, then sliding in the other direction.

- *Activities to develop hopping skills* include having students hop all the way around a hoop and hopping in and out of a hoop reversing direction. Students can also place ropes in straight lines and hop side-to-side over the rope from one end to the other and change (reverse) the direction.

- *Activities to develop skipping skills* include having student combine walking and hopping activities leading up to skipping.

- *Activities to develop stepping-hopping skills* include having students practice stepping and hopping activities while clapping hands to an uneven beat.

13.2 **Identify sequential development and activities for nonlocomotor skill acquisition.**

Sequential Development = stretch, bend, sit, shake, turn, rock and sway, swing, twist, dodge, and fall.

- *Activities to develop stretching* include lying on the back and stomach and stretching as long as possible; stretching as though one is reaching for a star, picking fruit off a tree, climbing a ladder, shooting a basketball, placing an item on a high shelf; waking and yawning.

- *Activities to develop bending* include touching knees and toes then straightening the entire body and straightening the body halfway; bending as though picking up a coin, tying shoes, picking flowers/vegetables, and petting animals of different sizes.

- *Activities to develop sitting* include practicing sitting from standing, kneeling, and lying positions without the use of hands.

- *Activities to develop falling skills* include first collapsing in one's own space and then pretending to fall like bowling pins, raindrops, snowflakes, a rag doll, and Humpty Dumpty.

13.3   Identify sequential development and activities for manipulative skill development.

<u>Sequential Development</u> = striking, throwing, kicking, ball-rolling, volleying, bouncing, catching, and trapping.

- *Activities to develop striking* include beginning with the object to be struck and the participant both being stationary. Next, the person remains still while trying to strike a moving object. Then, both the object and the participant are in motion as the participant attempts to strike the moving object.

- *Activities to develop throwing* include using yarn/foam balls and, first, throwing them against a wall; then at a big target; then at targets decreasing in size.

- *Activities to develop kicking* include alternating feet to kick balloons/beach balls; then kicking them under and over ropes; as proficiency develops, change the type of balls.

- *Activities to develop ball rolling* include rolling different size ball to a wall; then to targets decreasing in size.

- *Activities to develop volleying* include using a large balloon and, first, hitting it with both hands and then one hand (alternating hands) and then using different parts of the body. Change the object being volleyed as students progress (balloon to beach ball to foam ball etc.)

- *Activities to develop bouncing* includes starting with large balls and, first, using both hands to bounce; then using one hand (alternate hands).

- *Activities to develop catching* include using various objects (balloons, bean bags, balls, etc.) to catch and, first, catching the object the participant has thrown him/herself; then catching objects someone else threw and increasing the distance between the catcher and the thrower.

- *Activities to develop trapping* include trapping slow and fast rolling balls; trapping balls (or other objects such as bean bags) that are lightly thrown at waist, chest, and stomach levels; trapping different size balls.

Bibliography

Gallahue, David L. *Understanding Motor Development in Children.* New York: John Wiley & Sons, 1982.

Gallahue, David L. *Developmental Physical Education for Today's Children.* Dubuque, IA: Wm. C. Brown, 1993.

Hoffman. Hubert A., Jane Young, and Stephen Klesius. *Meaningful Movement for Children.* Boston: Allyn and Bacon, Inc., 1981.

Pica, Rae. *Experiences in Movement.* Albany, NY: Delmar Publishing, Inc., 1995.

Rink. Judith. *Teaching Physical Education for Learning.* St. Louis: Times Mirror/Mosby, 1985.

14.0 Knowledge of the analysis of motor performance.

14.1 Recognize errors in skill performance.

Because performing a skill has several components, determining why a participant is performing poorly may be difficult. Several attributes of a skill may have to be assessed to ascertain poor performance and, therefore, correct errors - if the skill can be broken down to measure a particular attribute at a time. **By observing a student's mechanical principles of motion while performing a skill, it would be reasonable to assume that the instructor should be able to identify performance errors.** This can be accomplished by using **process assessment** which is a subjective, observational approach to identify errors in the form, style, or mechanics of a skill.

14.2 Recognize appropriate objective measurements of fundamental skills.

Fundamental skills can be objectively measured by using **product assessments** which are quantitative measures of a movement's end result. How far, how fast, how high, or how many are the quantitative objectives of product assessments.

A **criterion-referenced test** (superior to a standardized test) or a **standardized norm-referenced test** can provide valid and reliable data for objectively measuring fundamental skills.

14.3 Use skill assessment information to correct errors in skill performance.

Diagnosing weakness to correct errors in skill performance can be formulated by using criterion-referenced standards since performance is usually evaluated by the level of achievement reached given proper instruction and ample practice. However, development of biomechanical instructional objectives could also be used.

Correcting errors in skill performance can be accomplished in the following activities:

- Archery - by measuring accuracy in shooting a standardized target from a specified place.

- Bowling - by calculating the bowling average attained under standardized conditions.

- Golf - by the score after several rounds.

- Swimming - by counting the number of breaststrokes needed to swim 25 yards.

Bibliography

Clarke, H. Harrison, and David H. Clarke. *Application of Measurement to Physical Education.* 6th ed. Englewood Cliffs, NJ: Prentice-Hall, 1987.

Gallahue, David L. *Developmental Physical Education for Today's Children.* 2nd ed. Dubuque, IA: Wm. C. Brown, 1993.

Kirkendall, Don R., Joseph J. Gruber, and Robert E. Johnson. *Measurement and Evaluation for Physical Educators.* 2nd ed. Champaign, IL: Human Kinetics, 1987.

15.0 Knowledge of rules, strategies, and terminology.

*Note: Because there are so many physical education activities, only some of them are covered in this section. It would be prudent to review all other physical education activities including, but not limited to, baseball, football, golf, softball, track, and wrestling.

15.1 Apply the rules of play to various game and sport situations.

Archery :

- Arrows that bounce off the target or go through the target count as 7 points.

- Arrows landing on lines between two rings receive the higher score of the two rings.

- Arrows hitting the petticoat receive no score.

Badminton :

- Intentionally balking opponent or making preliminary feints results in a fault (side in = loss of serve; side out = point awarded to side in).

- In bounds (fair play) when shuttlecock falls on a line.

- Striking team hits shuttlecock before it crosses net of striking team is a fault.

- A player touching the net when the shuttlecock is in play is a fault.

- The same player hitting the shuttlecock twice is a fault.

- The shuttlecock going through the net is a fault.

Basketball :

- A player touching the floor on or outside the boundary line is out-of-bounds.

- The ball is out of bounds if it touches anything (a player, the floor, an object, or any person) that is on or outside the boundary line.

- An offensive player remaining in the three second zone of the free-throw lane for more than three seconds is a violation.

- A ball firmly held by two opposing players or a defensive player closely guarding an offensive player with the ball for more than five seconds results in a jump ball.

- A throw-in is awarded to the opposing team of the last player touching a ball that goes out-of-bounds.

Bowling :

- No score for a pin knocked down by a pinsetter (human or mechanical).

- There is no score for the pins when any part of the foot, hand, or arm extends or crosses over the foul line (even after ball leaves the hand) or if any part of the body contacts division boards, walls, or uprights that are beyond the foul line.

- There is no count for pins displaced or knocked down by a ball leaving the lane before it reaches the pins.

- There is no count when balls rebound from the rear cushion.

Racquetball/Handball:

- A server stepping outside service area when serving faults.

- The server is out (relinquishes serve) if he/she steps outside of serving zone twice in succession while serving.

- Server is out if he/she fails to hit the ball rebounding off the floor during the serve.

- The opponent must have a chance to get placed or the referee must call for play before the server can serve the ball.

- The ball is re-served if the receiver is not behind the short line when the ball is served.

- A served ball that hits the front line and does not land back of the short line is "short"; therefore, it is a fault. The ball is also considered short when it hits the front wall and then two side-walls before it lands on the floor back of the short line.

- A serve is a fault when the ball touches the ceiling from rebounding off the front wall.

- A fault occurs when any part of the foot steps over the outer edges of the service or the short line while serving.

- A hinder (dead ball) is called when a returned ball hits an opponent on its way to the front wall - even if the ball continues to the front wall.

- Intentional or unintentional interference of an opponent having a chance to return the ball is a hinder.

Soccer:

The following are direct free kick offenses:

- Hand or arm contact with the ball,

- Using hands to hold an opponent,

- Pushing an opponent,

- Striking/kicking/tripping or attempting to strike/kick/trip an opponent;

- Goalie using the ball to strike an opponent,

- Jumping at or charging an opponent;

- Kneeing an opponent.

The following are indirect free kick offenses:

- Same player playing the ball twice at the kickoff, on a throw-in, on a goal kick, on a free kick, or on a corner kick.

- The goalie delaying getting rid of the ball or carrying the ball more than four steps.

- A referee not being notified of substitutions/re-substitutions and that player then handling the ball in the penalty area.

- Any person not a player entering playing field without a referee's permission.

- Disapproving actions or words of a referee's decision,

- Dangerously lowering the head or raising the foot too high to make a play,

- A player resuming play after being ordered off the field,

- Being "offside,"

- Attempting to kick the ball when the goalkeeper has possession or interference with the goalkeeper to hinder him/her from releasing the ball.

- Illegal charging;

- Leaving the playing field without referee's permission while the ball is in play.

Tennis:

A player loses a point when:

- The ball is allowed to bounce twice on player's side of the net.

- The ball is served or returned to any place outside designated areas.

- The ball is stopped by a player before it goes out-of-bounds.

- The ball is intentionally struck twice with the racket.

- Any part of a player or racket is struck by the ball after initial attempt to hit the ball.

- A player reaches over the net to hit the ball.

- A player throwing the racket at the ball.

- A ball striking any permanent fixture that is out-of-bounds (other than the net).

- Player is awarded a point after the service when the ball goes in the opponent's court without being returned after the ball touches the net or lands on a line.

Volleyball:

The following infractions by receiving team results in a point awarded to the serving side, and an infraction by serving team results in side-out:

- Illegal serves or serving out of turn,

- Illegal returns or catching or holding the ball,

- Dribbling or a player touching the ball twice in succession,

- Contact with the net,

- Touching the ball after it has been played three times without passing over the net,

- A player's foot completely touching the floor over the centerline,

- Reaching under the net and touching a player or the ball while the ball is in play,

- The players changing positions prior to the serve;

- Violating substitution or time-out regulations or delaying the game unnecessarily.

15.2 Apply appropriate strategies to game and sport situations.

Archery Strategies for correcting errors in aiming and releasing:

- Shifting position,

- Relaxing both the arms and shoulders at the moment of release,

- Not reaching point of aim before releasing string,

- Pointing aim to the right or left of direct line between the archer and the target's center,

- Aiming with the left eye,

- Sighting with both eyes;

- Using the wrong arrow.

Badminton Strategies:

Strategies for Return of Service:

- Returning serves with shots that are straight ahead,

- Returning service so that opponent moves out of his/her home base position,

- Returning long serves with an overhead clear or drop shot to near corner,

- Returning short serves with underhand clear or a net drop to near corner,

Strategies for Serving:

- Serving long to the backcourt near centerline,

- Serving short when opponent is standing too deep in his/her receiving court to return the serve, or using a short serve can be used to eliminate a smash return if opponent has a powerful smash from the backcourt.

Basketball Strategies:

Use a Zone Defense:

- To prevent drive-ins for easy lay-up shots,

- When playing area is small,

- When team is in foul trouble,

- To keep an excellent rebounder near opponent's basket,

- When opponents outside shooting is weak,

- When opponents have an advantage in height,

- When opponents have an exceptional offensive players, or when the best defenders cannot handle one-on-one defense,

Offensive Strategies Against Zone Defense:

- Using quick, sharp passing to penetrate zone forcing opposing player out of assigned position;

- Overloading and mismatching.

Offensive Strategies for One-On-One Defense:

- The "pick-and-roll" and the "give-and-go" are used to screen defensive players to get the ball open for an offensive player;

- Free-lancing (spontaneous one-one-one offense) can be used but, more commonly, "sets" of plays are used.

Bowling For Spares Strategies:

- Identifying the key pin and determining where it must be hit to pick up remaining pins,

- Using the three basic alignments: center position for center pins, left position for left pins, and right position for right pins,

- Rolling the spare ball in the same manner as rolled for the first ball of frame;

- Concentrating harder for spare ball since opportunity for pin action and margin of error are reduced.

Handball or Racquetball Strategies:

- Identifying opponent's strengths and weaknesses,

- Making opponent use less dominant hand or backhand shots when they are not developed and, therefore, a disadvantage;

- Frequently alternating fast balls and lobs to change the pace (changing the pace is particularly effective for serving),

- Maintaining position near middle of court (the well) that is close enough to play low balls and corner shots,

- Placing shots that keep opponent's position at a disadvantage to return cross court and angle shots,

- Using high lob shots that go overhead but do not hit the back wall with enough force to rebound to drive an opponent out of position when he/she persistently plays close to the front wall.

Soccer Strategies:

- *Heading* - using the head to pass, to shoot, or to clear the ball;

- *Tackling* - objective is to take possession of the ball from an opponent. Successful play requires knowledgeable utilization of space,

Tennis Strategies:

- Lobbing - the lob is used for defense that gives the player more time to get back into position,

- Identifying opponent's weaknesses and knowing one's own weaknesses to protect against them,

- Outrunning and out-thinking an opponent,

- Using change of pace, lob game, chop game, dashing to the net, and deception at the correct time.

Volleyball Strategies:

- Forearm Passes (bumps, digs, or passes) are used to play balls below the waist, to play balls that are driven hard, to pass the serve, and to contact distant balls from a player,

- Overhand Pass is used to accurately pass a ball above the head of a teammate and for setting techniques to pass the ball to an attacker;

- Attack Passes (drives, lobs, spikes) are used against opponent's aggressive play to keep opponent from returning the ball or to make a transition to return the ball aggressively.

15.3 Define the terminology of various physical education activities.

Archery Terminology:

- Addressing the target - Standing ready to shoot with a proper shooting stance.

- Anchor point - Specific location on the archer's face to which index finger comes while holding and aiming.

- Archery golf (adaptation of golf to archery) - Players shoot for holes scoring according to the number of shots required to hit the target.

- Arm guard - A piece of leather or plastic worn on the inside of the forearm is protecting the arm from the bowstring.

- Arrow plate - A protective piece of hard material set into the bow where the arrow crosses it.

- Arrow rest - A small projection at the top of the bow handle where the arrow rests.

- Back - The side of the bow away from the shooter,

- Bow arm - The arm that holds the bow.

- Bow sight - A device attached to the bow through which the archer sights when aiming.

- Bow weight - Designates the amount of effort needed to pull a bowstring a specific distance.

- Cant - Shooting while holding the bow slightly turned or tilted.

- Cast - The distance a bow can shoot an arrow.

- Clout shooting - A type of shooting using a target 48 feet in diameter that is laid on the ground at a distance of 180 yards for men and 120 or 140 yards for women. Usually 36 arrows are shot per round.

- Cock/Index feather - The feather that is set at a right angle to the arrow nock; differently colored than other two feathers.

- Creeping - Letting the drawing hand move forward at the release.

- Crest - The archer's identifying marks located just below the fletchings on the arrow.

- Draw - Pulling the bow string back into the anchor position.

- End - A specific number of arrows shot at one time or from one position before retrieval of arrows.

- Face - The part of the bow facing the shooter.

- Finger tab - A leather flap worn on the drawing hand protecting the fingers and providing a smooth release of the bow string.

- Fletchings - The feathers of the arrow which give guidance to its flight.

- Flight shooting- Shooting an arrow the farthest possible distance.

- Handle - The grip at the midsection of the bow.

- Hen feathers - The two feathers that are not set at right angles to the arrow nock.

- Instinctive shooting - Aiming and shooting instinctively rather than using a bow sight or point-of-aim method.

- Limbs - Upper and lower parts of the bow; divided by the handle.

- Nock - The groove in the arrow's end where the string is placed.

- Nocking point - The point on the string where the arrow is placed.

- Notch - The grooves of the upper and lower tips of the limbs where the bow string is fitted.

- Over bow - Using too strong a bow that is too powerful to pull a bowstring the proper distance.

- Overdraw - Drawing the bow so that the pile of the arrow is inside the bow.

- Petticoat - That part of the target face outside the white ring.

- Pile/point - The arrow's pointed metal tip.

- Plucking - Jerking the drawing hand laterally away from the face on the release causing the arrow's flight to the left.

- Point-blank range - The only distance from the target at which the point of aim is right on the bull's eye.

- Point-of-aim - A method of aiming that aligns the pile of the arrow with the target.

- Quiver - A receptacle for carrying or holding arrows.

- Recurve bow - A bow that is curved on the ends.

- Release - The act of letting the bowstring slip off the fingertips.

- Round - The term used to indicate shooting a specified number of arrows at a designated distance or distances.

- Roving - An outdoor archery game that uses natural targets (trees, bushes, stumps, etc.) for competition.

- Serving - The thread wrapped around the bowstring at the nocking point.

- Shaft - The long, body part of the arrow.

- Spine - The rigidity and flexibility characteristics of an arrow.

- Tackle - Archery equipment referred to in its entirety.

- Target face - The painted front of a target.

- Trajectory - The flight path of the arrow.

- Vane - An arrow's plastic feather.

Badminton Terminology:

- Alley - The area on each side of the court that is used for doubles that is 1.5 feet wide.

- Around-the-head stroke - An overhead stroke used to hit a forehand-like overhead stroke which is on the backhand side of the body.

- Back alley - The area between the baseline and the doubles long service line.

- Backcourt - The back third of the court.

- Backhand - A stroke made on the non-racket side of the body.

- Baseline - The back boundary line of the court.

- Bird - Another name for the shuttlecock/shuttle.

- Block - A soft shot used mainly to defend a smash; intercepting opponent's smash and returning it back over the net.

- Carry/Throw - A call when the shuttle remains on the racket during a stroke. It is legal if the racket follows the intended line of flight.

- Centerline - The mid-line separating the service courts.

- Clear - A high shot that going over the opponent's head and landing close to the baseline.

- Combination alignment - Partners playing both up-and-back and side-by-side during doubles games and./or volleys.

- Crosscourt - A diagonal shot hit into the opposite court.

- Defense - The team or player hitting the shuttle upwards.

- Double hit - An illegal shot where the shuttle is contacted twice by the racket in one swing.

- Doubles service court - The short, wide area to which the server must serve in doubles play.

- Down-the-line shot - A straight, ahead shot (usually down the sideline).

- Drive - A hard driven shot traveling parallel to the floor (clears net but does not have enough height for opponent to smash).

- Drop - A shot just clearing the net and then falling close to it.

- Face - The racket's string area.

- Fault - An infraction of the rules resulting in loss of serve or a point awarded to the server.

- First serve - A term used in doubles play to indicate that the server is the "first server" during an inning.

- Foot fault - Illegal movement/position of the feet by either the server or receiver.

- Forecourt - The front area of the court (between the net and the short service line).

- Forehand - A stroke made on the racket side of the body.

- Game point - The point, if won, that allows the server to win the game.

- Hand in - A term indicating that the server retains the serve.

- Hand out - The term used in doubles to denote that one player has lost the service.

- Home base - A center court position where a player can best play any shot hit by an opponent.

- Inning - The duration a player or team holds service.

- Let - Stopping the stopping because of some type of outside interference. The point is replayed.

- Lifting the shuttle - Stroking the shuttle underhanded and hitting it upward.

- Long serve - A high, deep serve landing near the long service line in doubles or the back boundary line in singles.

- Love - The term used to indicate a zero score.

- Match - A series of games. Winning two out of three games wins the match.

- Match point - The point, if won by the server, makes that person the winner of the match.

- Midcourt - The middle third of the court (between short service line and long service line for doubles).

- Net shot - A shot taken near the net.

- Non-racket side - The opposite side of the hand holding the racket.

- Offense - The team or player that is stroking the shuttle downward.

- Overhead - A motion used to strike the shuttle when it is above the head.

- Racket foot or leg - The foot or leg on the same side as the hand holding the racket.

- Ready position - The position a player assumes to be ready to move in any direction.

- Receiver - The player to whom the shuttle is served.

- Second serve - In doubles, the term indicates that one partner has lost the serve, and the other partner is now serving.

- Server - The player putting the shuttle into play.

- Setting - Choosing the amount of additional points to play when certain tie scores are reached.

- Short-serve - A serve barely clearing the net and landing just beyond the short service line.

- Shuttlecock/Shuttle - The feathered, plastic or nylon object which is volleyed back and forth over the net.

- Side Alley - See alley.

- Smash - An overhead stroke hit downward with great velocity and angle.

- "T" - The intersection of the centerline and the short service line.

- Underhand - A upward stroke to hit the shuttle when it has fallen below shoulder level.

- Unsight - illegal position taken by the server's partner so the receiver cannot see the shuttle being hit.

- Up-and-back - an offensive alignment used in doubles. The "up" player is responsible for the forecourt and the "back" player is responsible for both the midcourt and backcourt.

Basketball Terminology:

- Backcourt players (Guards) - Players who set up a team's offensive pattern.

- Backdoor - An offensive maneuver in which a player cuts toward the baseline to the basket, behind the defenders, and receives a ball for a field goal attempt.

- Baseline - The endline.

- Blocking/Boxing out - A term used when a player is positioned under the backboard to prevent an opposing player from achieving a good rebounding position.

- Charging - Personal contact by a player with the ball against the body of a defensive opponent.

- Corner players (Forwards) - Tall players that make up the sides of the offensive set-up who are responsible for the rebounding and shooting phases of the team's operation.

- Cut - A quick, offensive move by a player attempting to get free for a pass.

- Denial defense - Aggressive individual defense to keep an offensive player from receiving a pass.

- Double foul - Two opponents committing personal fouls against each other simultaneously.

- Dribble - ball movement by a player in control who throws or taps the ball in the air or onto the floor and then touches it. The dribble ends when the dribbler touches the ball with both hands concurrently, loses control, or permits it to come to rest while in contact with it.

- Drive - An aggressive move by a player with the ball toward the basket.

- Fake (Feint) - Using a deceptive move with the ball pulling the defensive player out of position.

- Fastbreak - Quickly moving the ball downcourt to score before the defense has a chance to set up.

- Field goal - A basket scored from the field.

- Freelance - No structure or set plays in the offense.

- Freethrow - The right given a player to score one or two points by unhindered shots for a goal from within the free throw circle and behind the free throw line.

- Give-and-go - A maneuver when the offensive player passes to a teammate and then immediately cuts in toward the basket for a return pass.

- Held ball - Occurs when two opponents have one or both hands firmly on the ball and neither can gain possession without undue roughness.

- Inside player (Center, Post, Pivot) - This player is usually the tallest team player who is situated near the basket, around the three-second lane area, and is responsible for rebounding and close-range shooting.

- Jump ball - A method of putting the ball into play by tossing it up between two opponents in the center circle to start the game or any overtime periods.

- Outlet pass - A term used that designates a direct pass from a rebounder to a teammate (the main objective is starting a fastbreak).

- Overtime period - An additional period of playing time when the score is tied at the end of the regulation game.

- Personal foul - A player foul which involves contact with an opponent while the ball is alive or after the ball is in possession of a player for a throw-in.

- Pick - A special type of screen where a player stands so the defensive player slides to make contact to free an offensive teammate for a shot or drive.

- Pivot - Occurs when a player who is holding the ball steps once or more than once in any direction with the same foot while the other foot, called the pivot foot, remains at its point of contact with the floor. Also, another term for the inside player.

- Posting up - A player cutting to the three-second lane area, pausing, and anticipating a pass.

- Rebound - When the ball bounces off the backboard or basket.

- Restraining circles - Three circles with a six-foot radius. One is located in the center of the court, and the others are located at each of the free-throw lines.

- Running time - Not stopping the clock for fouls or violations.

- Screen - An offensive maneuver positioning a player between the defender and a teammate to free the teammate for an uncontested shot.

- Switching - Defensive guards reversing their guarding assignments.

- Technical foul - A non-contact foul by a player, team, or coach for unsportsmanlike behavior or failing to abide by rules regarding submission of lineups, uniform numbering, and substitution procedures.

- Telegraphing a pass - A look or signal to indicate where the ball is going to be passed..

- Throw-in - A method of putting the ball in play from out-of-bounds.

- Traveling - Illegal progression of the ball, in any direction, of a player in possession of the ball within bounds.

- Violation - An infraction of the rules resulting in a throw-in from out-of-bounds.

Bowling Terminology:

- Anchor - The teammate who shoots last.

- Baby split - The 1-7 or 3-10 railroads.

- Backup - A reverse hook rotating to the right for a right-handed bowler.

- Bed posts - The 7-10 railroad.

- Blow - An error and missing a spare that is not split.

- Box - A frame.

- Brooklyn - A crossover ball striking the 1-2 pocket.

- Bucket - The 2-4-5-8 or 3-5-6-9 leaves.

- Cherry - Chopping off the front pin on a spare.

- Double - Two consecutive strikes.

- Double pinochle - The 7-6 and 4-10 split.

- Crossover - Same as a Brooklyn.

- Dutch 200 (Dutchman) - A score of 200 made by alternating strikes and spares for the entire game.

- Error - Same as a "blow."

- Foul - Touching or going beyond the foul line in delivering the ball.

- Frame - The box where scores are entered.

- Gutter ball - A ball that falls into either gutter.

- Handicap - Awarding an individual or team a bonus score or score adjustment that is based on averages.

- Head pin - The number one pin.

- Hook - A ball that breaks to the left for a right-handed bowler and breaks to the right for a left-handed bowler.

- Jersey side - Same as a Brooklyn.

- Kegler - Synonym bowler.

- Lane - A bowling alley.

- Leave - Pin or pins left standing after a throw.

- Light hit - Hitting the head pin lightly to the right or left side.

- Line - A complete game as recorded on the score sheet.

- Mark - Getting a strike or spare.

- Open frame - A frame in which no mark is made and leaving at least one pin standing after rolling both balls in a frame.

- Pocket - Space between the head pin and pins on either side.

- Railroad - Synonym for a split.

- Sleeper - A pin hidden from view.

- Spare - Knocking all pins down with two balls.

- Split - A leave, after throwing the first ball, in which the number one pin plus a second pin are down, and seven pins remain standing.

- Spot - A bowler's point of aim on the alley.

- Striking out - Obtaining three strikes in the last frame.

- Tap - A pin that remains standing after an apparently perfect hit.

- Turkey - Three consecutive strikes.

Racquetball/Handball Terminology:

- Ace - A serve that completely eludes the receiver.

- Back wall shot - A shot made from a rebound off the back wall.

- Box - See service box.

- Ceiling shot - A shot that first strikes the ceiling, then the front wall.

- Crotch - The junction of any two playing surfaces, as between the floor and any wall.

- Crotch shot - A ball that simultaneously strikes the front wall and floor (not good).

- Cut throat - A three-man game in which the server plays against the other two players. Each player keeps an individual score.

- Drive shot - A power shot against the front wall rebounding in a fast, low, and straight line.

- Fault - An illegally served ball.

- Handout - Retiring the server who fails to serve legally or when the serving team fails to return a ball that is in play.

- Hinder - Interference or obstruction of the flight of the ball during play.

- Kill - A ball rebounded off the front wall so close to the floor that it is impossible to return.

- Passing shot - A shot placed out an opponent's reach on either side.

- Rally - Continuous play of the ball by opponents.

- Receiving line - The broken line parallel to the short line on a racquetball court.

- Run-around shot - A ball striking one side wall, the rear wall, and the other side wall.

- Safety zone - A five-foot area bounded by the back edge of the short line and receiving line that is only observed during the serve in racquetball.

- Screen - A hinder due to obstruction of the opponent's vision.

- Server - Person in the "hand-in" position and eligible to serve.

- Service box - The service zone bounded by the side wall and a parallel line 18 inches away; denotes where server's partner must stand in doubles during the serve.

- Service court - The area where the ball must land when it is returned from the front wall on the serve.

- Service line - The line that is parallel to and five feet in front of the short line.

- Service zone - The area where the ball must be served.

- Short line - The line on the floor parallel to front wall and equidistant from front and back wall. The serve must go over this line when returning from the front wall.

- Shoot - Attempting kill shots.

- Side out - Losing the serve.

- Throng - The strap on the bottom handle of the racquetball racquet which is worn around the player's wrist.

- Volley - Returning the ball to the front wall before it bounces on the floor.

- Z-ball - A defensive shot that strikes the front wall, a sidewall, and then the opposite side wall.

Soccer Terminology:

- Center - Passing from the outside of the field near the side line into the center.

- Charge - Illegal or legal body contact between opponents.

- Chip - Lofting the ball into the air using the instep kick technique: contacting the ball very low causing it to loft quickly with back spin.

- Clear - Attempting to move the ball out of danger by playing the ball a great distance.

- Corner kick - A direct free kick from the corner arc awarded to the attacking player when the defending team last played the ball over their own end line.

- Cross - a pass from the outside of the field near the end line to a position in front of the goal.

- Dead ball situation - The organized restarting of the game after stopping the play.

- Direct free kick - A free kick whereby the kicker may score immediately from that initial contact.

- Dribble - The technique of a player self-propelling the ball with the foot in order to maintain control of the ball while moving from one spot to another.

- Drop ball - The method used to restart the game after temporary suspension of play when the ball is still playable.

- Goal area - The rectangular area in front of the goal where the ball is placed for a goal kick.

- Half-volley - Contacting the ball just as it hits the ground after being airborne.

- Head - Playing the ball with the head.

- Indirect free kick - A free kick from which player, other than the kicker, must contact the ball before a score can be made.

- Kickoff - The free kick starting play at the beginning of the game, after each period, or after a score.

- Obstruction - Illegally using the body to shield an opponent from reaching the ball.

- One-touch - immediately passing a received ball without stopping it.

- Penalty area - The large rectangular area in front of the goal where the goalkeeper is allowed to use the hands to play the ball.

- Penalty kick - A free kick awarded in the penalty area against the defending team for a Direct Free Kick foul.

- Settle - Taking a ball that is off the ground and getting it settled on the ground so that it is rolling and no longer bouncing.

- Square pass - A pass directed toward the side of a player.

- Tackle - A technique to take the ball away from the opponents.

- Through pass - A pass penetrating between and past the defenders.

- Throw-in - The technique to restart the game when the ball goes out of play over the side line.

- Touchline - The side line of the field.

- Trap - The technique used for receiving the ball and bringing it under control.

- Two-touch- receiving - Trapping and immediately re-passing the ball.

Tennis Terminology:

- Ace - Serving a ball untouched by the opponent's racket.

- Advantage (Ad) - A scoring term. The next point won after the score is "deuce."

- Alley - The 4.5 foot strip on either side of the singles court that is used to enlarge the court for doubles.

- Approach shot - A shot hit inside the baseline while approaching the net.

- Backcourt - The area between the service line and the baseline.

- Backhand - Strokes that are hit on the left side of a right-handed player.

- Backspin - Spin acquired on a ball dropping from a vertical position forcing the ball to bounce back toward the hitter.

- Backswing - The beginning of all ground strokes and service motion requiring a backswing to gather energy for the forward swing.

- Baseline - The end line of a tennis court.

- Break - Winning a game in which the opponent serves.

- Center mark - A short mark bisecting the baseline.

- Center service line - The perpendicular line to the net dividing the two service courts in halves.

- Center strap - The strap at the center of the net that is anchored to the court to facilitate a constant 3-foot height for the net at its center.

- Center stripe - Same as the center service line.

- Chip - A short chopping motion of the racket against the back and bottom side of the ball.

- Chop - Placing backspin on the ball with a short, high-to-low, forward swing.

- Cross-court - A shot hit diagonally from one corner of the court over the net into the opposite corner of the court.

- Cut off the angle - Moving forward quickly against an opponent's cross-court shot, allowing the player to hit the ball near the center of the court rather than near the sidelines.

- Deep (depth) - A shot bouncing near the baseline on ground strokes and near the service line on serves.

- Default - A player who forfeits his/her position in a tournament by not playing a scheduled match.

- Deuce - A term used when the game score is 40-40.

- Dink - A ball hit very softly and relatively high to ensure its safe landing.

- Double fault - Two consecutive out-of-bound serves on the same point.

- Doubles line - The outside sidelines on a court used only for doubles.

- Down-the-line - A shot hit near a sideline traveling close to, and parallel to, the same line from which the shot was initially hit.

- Drive - An offensive shot hit with extra force.

- Drop shot - A ground stroke hit so that it drops just over the net with little or no forward bounce.

- Drop volley - A volley hit in such a manner that it drops just over the net with little or no forward bounce.

- Error - A mistake made by a player during competition.

- Flat shot - A ball hit so there is no rotation when traveling through the air.

- Foot fault - Illegal foot movement before service penalized by losing that particular serve. Common foot faults are: stepping on or ahead of the baseline before the ball has been contacted, and running along the baseline before serving.

- Forecourt - The area between the net and the service line.

- Forehand - The stroke hit on the right side of a right-handed player.

- Frame - The rim of the racket head plus the handle of the racket.

- Game - Scoring term when a player wins 4 points before an opponent while holding a minimum 2-point lead.

- Grip - The portion of the racket that is grasped in the player's hand.

- Ground stroke - Any ball hit after it has bounced.

- Half-volley - A ball hit inches away from the court's surface after the ball bounced.

- Hold serve - Winning your own serve. If you lose your own serve, your serve has been "broken."

- Let (ball) - A point replayed because of some kind of interference.

- Let serve - A serve that touches the net tape, falls into the proper square, and is played over.

- Linesman - A match official who calls balls "in" or "out."

- Lob - A ball hit with sufficient height to pass over the out-stretched arm position of the net player.

- Lob volley - A shot hit high into the air from a volleying position.

- Love - Scoring term that means zero points or games.

- Match - A contest between two or four opponents.

- Match point - The point immediately before the final point of a match.

- Midcourt - The area in front or in back of the service line of the playing court.

- Net ball - A ball that hits the net falling on the same side as the hitter.

- No man's land - A general area within the baseline and proper net position area. When caught in that area, the player must volley or hit ground strokes near his/her feet.

- Offensives lob - A ball hit just above the racket reach of an opposing net player.

- Open face racket - A racket whose face is moving under the ball. A wide open racket face is parallel to the court surface.

- Overhead - A shot hit from a position higher than the player's head.

- Overhitting - Exerting too much force into each shot.

- Pace - The speed of the ball.

- Passing shot - A shot passing beyond the reach of the net player landing inbounds.

- Placement - A shot hit inbounds that is untouched by the opponent.

- Poach - To cross over into your partner's territory.

- Racket face - The racket's hitting surface.

- Racket head - The top portion of the racket frame which houses the strings.

- Rally - Opponents hitting balls back and forth across the net.

- Receiver - The player about to return the opponent's serve.

- Retrieve - An excellent defensive shot in response to an opponent's well-placed offensive shot.

- Server - The player initiating play.

- Service line - The line at the end of the service courts parallel to the net.

- Set - A scoring term meaning the first player to win six games with a minimum two-game lead has won a set.

- Set point - The point, if won, which will give the player the set.

- Sidespin - A ball hit rotating on a horizontal plane.

- Signals in doubles - Signaling your partner that you are going to poach at the net.

- Singles line - The sideline closest to the center mark that runs the entire length of the court.

- Slice - Motion of the racket head going around the side of the ball producing a horizontal spin on ball.

- Tape - The band of cloth or plastic running across the top of the net.

- Telegraphing the play - Indicating the direction of one's intended target before hitting the ball.

- Topspin - The clockwise rotation of the ball at a 90 degree angle.

- Touch - The ability to make delicate, soft shots from several positions on the court.

- Twist - A special rotation applied to the ball during the serve causing the ball to jump to the left (of right-handed server).

- Umpire - The official that calls lines.

- Underspin - A counterclockwise spin placed on the ball.

- Volley - Hitting the ball in the air before it bounces on the court.

Volleyball Terminology:

- Attack - Returning the ball across the net in an attempt to put the opponents at a disadvantage.

- Ball handling - Executing any passing fundamental.

- Block - Intercepting the ball just before or as it crosses the net.

- Bump - See forearm pass.

- Court coverage - Defensive player's court assignment.

- Dig - An emergency pass usually used to defend a hard-driven attack.

- Dink - A soft shot off the fingertips to lob the ball over a block.

- Double foul - Infraction of rules by both teams during the same play.

- Drive - An attack contacted in the center that attempts to hit the ball off the blocker's hands.

- Fault - Any infraction of the rules.

- Forearm pass - A pass made off the forearms that is used to play served balls, hard-driven spikes, or any low ball.

- Free ball - A ball that is returned by the opponent that may easily be handled.

- Front court - The playing area where it is legal to block or attack.

- Held ball - A ball that is simultaneously contacted above the net by opponents and momentarily held upon contact.

- Kill - An attack that cannot be returned.

- Lob - A soft attack contacted on the back bottom quarter of the ball causing its trajectory upward.

- Overhand pass - A pass made by contacting the ball above the head with the finger pads.

- Overlap - An illegal foot position, when the ball is dead, with an adjacent player putting another out of position.

- Play over - Replaying the rally because of a held ball or the official prematurely suspending play. The server re-serves with no point awarded.

- Point - A point is scored when the receiving team fails to legally return the ball to the opponents' court.

- Rotation - Clockwise rotation of the players upon gaining the ball from the opponents.

- Serve - Putting the ball in play over the net by striking it with the hand.

- Set - Placing the ball near the net to facilitate attacking.

- Setter - The player assigned to set the ball.

- Side out - Side is out when the serving team fails to win a point or plays the ball illegally.

- Spike - A ball hit with top spin and with a strong downward force into the opponents' court.

- Spiker - The player assigned to attack the ball.

- Spike-roll - An attack that first takes an upward trajectory using the spiking actions (with or without jumping).

- Topspin (Overspin) - Applying forward spin to the ball during the serve, spike, or spike roll.

15.4 Apply appropriate officiating techniques to sport situations.

*NOTE: Since rules change yearly, acquiring new rule books every year is necessary for proper officiating.

- Basketball situation: Actions of the spectators interfere with the progression of the game.
  Ruling: An official may call a foul on whatever team's supporters who are interfering with the game.

- Basketball situation: A1 is attempting a field goal and is fouled by B1. A1 continues with the field goal attempt and before releasing the ball crashes into B2, who has legal position on the floor. A1 successfully completes the field goal.
  Ruling: The ball was immediately dead when A1 fouled B2; therefore, field goal does not count. However, since A1 was fouled by B1 while attempting the field goal, A1 is awarded two free throws.

- Basketball situation: The official in the front court runs into a pass thrown from the back court by A1 and goes out-of-bounds.
  Ruling: Throw-in is awarded to B.

- Basketball Situation: A1 catches the ball in mid-air and lands with the right foot first and then the left foot. A1 pivots on the left foot.
  Ruling: A violation has occurred because A1 can only pivot on the foot that first lands on the floor which was the right foot.

- Soccer situation: The ball is alive when a substitute enters the playing field.
  Ruling: A non-player foul. Referee can either penalize at location of the next dead ball or at the place of entry (usually where the team that is offended is at an advantage).

- Soccer situation: A1 goalie, in own penalty area, is charged by B1.
  Ruling: Team A is awarded a Direct free-kick at the spot of foul. A flagrant charge awards team A a penalty-kick at the other end of the field, and B1 is disqualified.

- Soccer situation: The goalie is out of position when a back on team B heads the ball out and falls into the net. A2 gets the ball, passes it to A1, and has only the goalie to beat.
  Ruling: A1 is not offside because the B back left the field during legal play.

- Volleyball situation: Team A second volley hits an obstruction directly over the net, returns to A's playing area, and is again played by team A.
  Ruling: Fair play and the next play is team A's third play.

- Volleyball situation: The serving team has three front line players standing close together in front of the server at the spiking line.
  Ruling: Illegal alignment is called for intentional screening.

- Volleyball situation: RB and CB on the receiving team are overlapping when the ball is contacted for the serve, and the serve lands out-of-bounds.
  Ruling: Serving team is awarded a point because of receiving team's illegal alignment.

- Volleyball situation: LB on team B saves a spiked ball and it deflects off his/her shoulder.
  Ruling: A legal hit.

Bibliography

Clegg, Richard, and William A. Thompson. *Modern Sports Officiating.* 2nd ed. Dubuque, IA: Wm. C. Brown, 1979.

Dolan, Edward F. *Calling the Play.* New York: McClelland and Stewart Ltd., 1982.

Mood, Dale, Frank F. Musker, and Judith E. Rink. *Sports and Recreational Activities.* 9th ed. St. Louis: Times Mirror/Mosby, 1987.

Seaton, Don Cash, Neil Schmottlach, Jerre L. McManama, Irene A. Clayton, Howard C. Leibee, and Lloyd L. Messesmith. *Physical Education Handbook.* 8th ed. Englewood Cliffs, NJ: Prentice-Hall, 1992.

16.0 Knowledge of appropriate behavior in physical education activities.

1. Appropriate Student Etiquette/Behaviors include: following the rules and accepting the consequences of unfair action. good sportsmanship, respecting the rights of other students, reporting own accidents and mishaps, not engaging in inappropriate behavior under peer pressure encouragement, cooperation, paying attention to instructions and demonstrations, moving to assigned places and remaining in own space. complying with directions, practicing as instructed to do so, properly using equipment: not interfering with the practice of others.

2. Appropriate Content Etiquette/Behaviors include: the teacher describing the performance of tasks and students engaging in the task, the teacher assisting students with task performance, and the teacher modifying and developing tasks.

3. Appropriate Management Etiquette/Behaviors include: the teacher directing the management of equipment, students, and space prior to practicing tasks; students getting equipment and partners; teacher requesting cessation of "fooling around."

Bibliography

Rink, Judith E. *Teaching Physical Education for Learning.* St. Louis: Times Mirror/Mosby, 1985.

Siedentop, Daryl. *Physical Education: Teaching and Curriculum Strategies for Grades 5-12.* Palo Alto, CA: Mayfield.

17.0   Knowledge of instructional strategies.

17.1   Identify techniques to enhance skill and strategy performance.

Playing complex games requires preparing individuals to combine skills, using skills in a more complex way, and relating to others in both offensive and defensive associations. Developing these abilities can be regarded as having fours stages.

Stage One concerns **controlling an object.** For striking or throwing objects, individuals can consistently practice sending object's to a specified location developing control of the force that intentionally accomplishes the objective. For catching or collecting, individuals can practice control by securing possession of an object from any direction, level, or speed. For carrying and propelling, individuals can practice maintaining control of an object by moving in different directions and at different paces. Developing control begins first by providing easy attainment of the objective(s) and gradually increasing the difficulty by modifying the direction, the level, and the force, as well as changing from a stationary position to moving.

Stage Two still is concerned with controlling an object; however, **difficulty is added** by combining skills and using them with the interaction of others. Rules are stressed to constrain the execution of skills. Drills such as passing and dribbling can develop stage two.

Stage Three focuses on **offense and defense** utilizing correct skill performance. Students should now be able to control objects; therefore, the focus shifts to obtaining and maintaining possession as well as offensive and defensive strategies in the midst of opponents. Net activities and keep-away games help develop this stage as well as adding more offensive and defensive players, adding boundaries, keeping score, and enforcing conduct rules. Students develop adjusting their responses with each element introduced to the activity.

Stage Four encounters **complex activity.** The complete activity is executed as well as modified activities to assist students to achieve participation at this stage. Continuous play is important; thus, the instructor may have to modify rules or a part of the activity to keep flow of game constant (i.e. eliminating free throws/kicks, substituting volleyball serve with a throw; initiating play out-of-bounds).

17.2   Identify types of tournaments, meets, and game organizations.

The types of tournaments include: single elimination, round robin, double elimination, ladder, pyramid, and spiderweb.

The types of meets include: intramural, extramural, and interscholastic sports clubs.

Games can be organized by: grade levels, homerooms, clubs, societies, physical education classes, study groups, age, height, weight, residential districts, or by arbitrary assignment of groups by staff.

17.3 **Identify teaching methods, techniques, and aids that facilitate cognitive and psychomotor learning.**

Teaching methods that facilitate cognitive learning include:

1. Problem Solving - The instructor presents the initial task, and students come to an acceptable solution in unique and divergent ways.

2. Conceptual Theory - The instructor's focus is on acquisition of knowledge.

3. Guided Guided/Inquiry - goal is reached by careful stages of instructions strategically guiding students through a sequence of experiences.

Initially, performing skills will be variable, inconsistent, error prone, "off-time," and awkward. Students' focus will be on remembering what to do. Errors in gross movement need to be directed at the significant elements of the skill, and clear information of the skill's biomechanics should be emphasized. So students will not be overburdened with too much information, one or two elements at a time should be performed. Motivation occurs with supportive and encouraging comments.

Techniques to facilitate cognitive learning include:

1. Transfer of learning - identifying similar movements of a previous learned skill and the new skill.

2. Planning for slightly longer instructions and demonstrations as students memorize cues and skills.

3. Using appropriate language for the level of the students.

4. Conceptual Thinking - giving those students' more responsibility for their learning who are capable of doing so.

Aids to facilitate cognitive learning include:

1. Assessing students' performance frequently.

2. Moving activities incorporating principles of biomechanics.

3. Using laser discs; computers and software.

4. Videotaping students' performance.

Teaching methods to facilitate psychomotor learning include:

1. Task/Reciprocal - The instructor programs task learning into the learning setting by utilizing stations.

2. Command/Direct - Task instruction is teacher-centered in which goals are clear, skills are explained and demonstrated, time is allocated for practice, and students' performance is frequently monitored.

3. Contingency/Contract - A task style of instruction that rewards completion of tasks.

Techniques that facilitate psychomotor learning include:

1. <u>Reflex movements</u> - Activities that create an automatic response to some stimuli. Responses encompass flexing, extending, stretching, and postural adjustment.

2. <u>Basic fundamental locomotor movements</u> - Activities that utilize instinctive patterns of movement established by combining reflex movements.

3. <u>Perceptual abilities</u> - Activities that involve interpreting auditory, visual, tactile stimuli in order to coordinate adjustments.

4. <u>Physical abilities</u> - Activities to develop physical characteristics of fitness providing students with the stamina necessary for highly advanced, skilled movement.

5. <u>Skilled movements</u> - Activities that involve instinctive, effective performance of complex movement including vertical and horizontal components.

6. <u>Nondiscursive communication</u> - Activities necessitating expression as part of the movement.

17.4 Apply student and program evaluations to redesigning instructional strategies in physical education.

The **Cheffers Adaptation of the Flanders Interaction Analysis System** (CAFAIS) and the **Academic Learning Time in Physical Education** (ALT-PE) are *Systematic Analyses* that detect continuous and discrete behaviors, actions and interactions, and teaching characteristics. Presenting the goals of a Systematic Analysis to the data obtained of the instructional processes can indicate which of the following instructional strategies need changing:

- The ability of the teacher to question and the time engaged in questioning.

- The cognitive response of students.

- The time spent on task instruction (rate per minute).

- The number of times task instruction takes place (rate of occurrence).

The following **Systematic Observational Evaluations** can be used to identify changes that need to be made in events, in duration, in groups, and in self recording:

- **Event Recording** (rate per minute; rate of occurrence) - The number of attempts students have to try a skill and the number of the teacher's positive interactions with the students are counted.

- **Duration Recording** - Measures amount of time teacher spends on instructions, time spent on managing students' activities, and time spent managing the participation of students.

- **Group Time Sampling/Placheck Recording** - The number of students participating in the activity are counted;

- **Self Recording** - Students sign in their arrival time to class and how many completed tasks they accomplished.

The **Reflective Approach** evaluation is continuous self-monitoring by the teacher. him/herself, of situations, behaviors, practices, effectiveness, and accomplishments. These variables are compared with the harmonious temperament of particular situations to identify where changes are necessary.

Student assessments that can facilitate changes in instructional strategies include:

- **Formal assessments** such as win/loss records, written tests, skills tests, performance records, and reviewing videotaped performances.

- **Informal assessments** such as rating scales, observational performance descriptions, completion of skills checklist, and observational time utilization.

Bibliography

Bucher, Charles A. *Management of Physical Education and Athletic Training Programs.* 9th ed. St. Louis: Times Mirror/Mosby, 1987.

Bucher, Charles A., and C. R. Koenig. *Methods and Materials For Secondary School Physical Education.* 6th ed. St. Louis: Times Mirror/Mosby, 1983.

Horine, Larry. *Administration of Physical Education and Sports Programs.* Philadelphia: Saunders College Publishing, 1985.

Mohnsen, Bonnie S. *Using Technology in Physical Education.* Champaign, IL: Human Kinetics, 1995.

Pangrazi, Robert P., and Paul W. Darst. *Dynamic Physical Education Curriculum and Instruction for Secondary School Students.* Minneapolis: Burgess Publishing Company, 1985.

Rink, Judith E. *Teaching Physical Education for Learning.* St. Louis: Times Mirror/Mosby, 1985.

Seaton, Don Cash, Neil Schmottlach, Jerre L. McManama, Irene A. Clayton, Howard C. Leibee, and Lloyd L. Messesmith. *Physical Education Handbook.* 8th ed. Englewood Cliffs, NJ: Prentice-Hall, 1992.

Siedentop, Daryl. *Physical Education: Teaching and Curriculum Strategies for Grades 5-12.* Palo Alto, CA: Mayfield, 1986.

Wessel, Janet A., and Luke Kelly. *Achievement - Based Curriculum Development in Physical Education.* Philadelphia: Lea & Febiger, 1986.

Wuest, Deborah A., and Bennett J. Lombardo. *Curriculum and Instruction: The Secondary School Physical Education Experience.* St. Louis: Mosby, 1994.

18.0   Knowledge of physical fitness components.

18.1   Identify the health-related components of physical fitness.

There are five health related components of physical fitness: *cardiorespiratory or cardiovascular endurance, muscle strength, muscle endurance, flexibility, and body composition.*

Cardiorespiratory/Cardiovascular Endurance is the ability of the heart, blood vessels, circulatory and respiratory systems to supply fuel, especially oxygen, to the muscles during sustained exercise or work.

Muscle Strength is the force that a muscle or group of muscles exert against a resistance in one maximal effort/single muscle contraction.

Muscle Endurance is the ability of the muscles to repeatedly contract over a period of time without undue fatigue.

Flexibility is the functional capacity of a joint or series of joints to move through a full range of motion.

Body Composition is the proportion of the percent of lean body mass and the percent of body fat that comprise body weight.

18.2   Identify the skill related components of physical fitness.

The skill related components of physical fitness are *agility, balance, coordination, power, reaction time, and speed.*

Agility the ability to quickly change direction of the body with speed and accuracy.

Balance is the ability to maintain equilibrium while the body is stationary or moving.

Coordination is the ability to use the senses (i.e. sight and hearing) in conjunction with the body/body parts to perform smooth and accurate motor tasks.

Power is the rate at which a person can execute a movement within a short period of time.

Reaction Time is the time elapsed between a stimulation and the starting of a person's reaction to it.

Speed is the ability to execute a movement within a short period of time.

18.3   Select valid physical fitness test items to measure health and skill related fitness components.

Cardiorespiratory fitness can be measured by the following tests: maximal stress test, submaximal stress test, Bruce Protocol, Balke Protocol, Astrand and Rhyming Test, PWC Test, Bench Step Test, Rockport Walking Fitness Test; Cooper 1.5 Mile Run/Walk Fitness Test.

Muscle strength can be measured by the following: dynamometers (hand. back, and leg), cable tensiometer. The 1-RM Test (repetition maximum: bench press, standing press, arm curl, and leg press), Bench Squat Test, Sit-Up Test (one sit up holding a weight plate behind the neck); Lateral Pull-Down.

Muscle endurance can be assessed by the following: Squat Thrust Test, Pull-Ups Test, Sit-Ups Test, Lateral Pull-Down. Bench-Press Test, Arm Curl, push-ups; dips.

Flexibility can be measured by the following tests: sit and reach, Kraus-Webber Floor Touch Test, Trunk Extension, Forward Bend of Trunk Test, Leighton Flexometer, shoulder rotation/flexion test; goniometer.

Body Composition can be determined by the following: Hydrostatic Weighing, Skinfold Measurements, limb/girth circumference, and body mass index.

Agility can be assessed with The Illinois Agility Run.

Balance can be evaluated with the following: The Bass Test of Dynamic Balance (lengthwise and crosswise), the Johnson Modification of the Bass Test of Dynamic Balance, modified sideward leap; balance beam walk.

Coordination can be assessed by The Stick test of Coordination.

Power can be measured by the vertical jump.

Speed can be assessed with the 50 yard dash.

Bibliography

Baumgartner, Ted A. and Andrew S. Jackson. *Measurement for Evaluation in Physical Education and Exercise Science.* 3rd ed. Dubuque, IA: Wm. C. Brown Publishers, 1987.

Corbin, Charles B., and Lindsey, Ruth. *Concepts of Physical Fitness.* 8th ed. Dubuque, IA: Wm. C. Brown, 1994.

Donatelle, Rebecca, Christine Snow-Harter, and Anthony Wilcox. *Wellness Choices for Health and Fitness.* Redwood City, CA: The Benjamin/Cummings Publishing Company, Inc., 1995.

Heyward, Vivian H. *Designs for Fitness.* Minneapolis: Burgess Publishing Company, 1984.

Kusenity, Ivan and Morton Fine. *Your Guide To Getting Fit.* Mountain View, CA: Mayfield Publishing Company, 1987.

Lindsey, Ruth, Billie J. Jones, and Ada Van Whitley. *Fitness for the Health of It.* 6th ed. Dubuque, IA: Wm. C. Brown, 1989.

McArdle, William D., Frank I. Katch, and Victor L. Katch. *Essentials of Exercise Physiology.* Philadelphia: Lea & Febiger, 1994.

Neiman, David C. *The Sports Medicine Fitness Course.* Palo Alto, CA: Bull Publishing Company.

Rosato. Frank D. *Fitness for Wellness: The Physical Connection.* 3rd ed. Minneapolis/St. Paul: West Publishing Company, 1994.

Safrit, Margret J., and Terry M. Wood. *Introduction to Measurement in Physical Education and Exercise Science.* 3rd ed. St. Louis: Times Mirror/Mosby, 1995.

Stokes. Roberta and Clancy Moore. *Personal Fitness and You.* 3rd ed. Winston-Salem, NC: Hunter, 1993.

Williams. Charles, Emmanouel G. Harageones, DeWayne J. Johnson, and Charles D. Smith. *Personal Fitness: Looking Good/Feeling Good.* Dubuque, IA: Kendall/Hunt, 1984.

19.0 Knowledge of exercise training principles.

19.1 Identify basic training principles.

The *Overload Principle* is exercising at a level above normal to improve a physical or physiologic capacity (working a load that is more than normal).

The *Specificity Principle* is overloading specifically for a particular fitness component. In order for a component of fitness to be improved, it must be, specifically worked on. Metabolic and physiologic adaptations are dependent on the type of overload; hence, specific exercise produces specific adaptations creating specific training effects.

The *Progression Principle* states that once the body adapts to the original load/stress, no further improvement of a component of fitness will occur unless an additional load is added.

There is also a *Reversibility-of-Training Principle* in which all gains in fitness will be lost with the discontinuance of a training program.

19.2 Identify the variables by which overload can be modified.

Overload can be modified by varying *frequency, intensity, and time.*

Frequency is how many times per week/number of exercise sessions included in an exercise program.

Intensity is how hard one is working/exercising.

Time/Duration is how many minutes that the proper intensity level of exercise is maintained.

19.3 Compute the target heart rate zone.

There are three ways to calculate the target heart rate. Target heart rate (THR) can be calculated by:

1. METs (maximum oxygen uptake) which is 60% to 90% of functional capacity.

2. Karvonean Formula = (MHR - RHR) x intensity + RHR.
   MHR= 220 - Age;
   RHR = Resting heart range;
   Intensity = Target Heart Range (which is 60% - 80% of MHR - RHR + RHR). **THR = (MHR - RHR) x .60 + RHR to (MHR - RHR) x .80 + RHR**

3. Cooper's Formula to determine target heart range is:
   THR = (220 - AGE) x .60 to (220 - AGE) x .80.

19.4 **Identify how the health-related components of physical fitness may be improved by implementing the principles of overload, progression, and specificity.**

1. **Cardiorespiratory Fitness:**

Overloading for cardiorespiratory fitness:

- Frequency = minimum of 3 days/week

- Intensity = exercising in target heart rate zone;

- Time = minimum of 15 minutes rate.

Progression for cardiovascular fitness:

- Begin at a frequency of 3 days/week and work up to no more than 6 days/week,

- Begin at an intensity near THR threshold and work up to 80% of THR;

- Begin at 15 minutes and work up to 60 minutes.

Specificity for cardiovascular fitness:

- To specifically develop cardiovascular fitness, aerobic (with oxygen) activities must be performed for at least fifteen minutes without developing an oxygen debt. Aerobic activities include, but are not limited to: brisk walking, jogging, bicycling, and swimming.

2. **Muscle Strength:**

Overloading for muscle strength:

- Frequency = every other day,

- Intensity = 60% to 90% of assessed muscle strength;

- Time = 3 sets of 3 - 8 reps (high resistance with a low number of repetitions).

Progression for muscle strength:

- Begin 3/days week and work up to every other day,

- Begin near 60% of determined muscle strength and work up to no more than 90% of muscle strength,

- Begin with 1 set with 3 reps and work up to 3 sets with 8 reps.

Specificity for muscle strength:

- To increase muscle strength for a specific part(s) of the body, that/those part(s) of the body must be targeted.

3. **Muscle endurance:**

Overloading for muscle endurance:

- Frequency = every other day,

- Intensity = 30% to 60% of assessed muscle strength,

- Time = 3 sets of 12 - 20 reps (low resistance with a high number of repetitions).

Progression for muscle endurance:

- Begin 3 days/week and work up to every other day,

- Begin at 20% to 30% of muscle strength and work up to no more than 60% of muscle strength,

- Begin with 1 set with 12 reps and work up to 3 sets with 20 reps.

Specificity for muscle endurance:

- Same as muscle strength.

4. **Flexibility:**

Overloading for flexibility:

- Frequency: 3 to 7 days/week,

- Intensity: stretch muscle beyond its normal length,

- Time: 3 sets of 3 reps holding stretch 15 to 60 seconds.

Progression for flexibility:

- Begin 3 days/week and work up to every day,

- Begin stretching with slow movement as far as possible without pain holding at the end of the range of motion (ROM) and work up to stretching no more than 10% beyond the normal ROM,

- Begin with 1set with 1rep holding stretches 15 seconds and work up to 3 sets with 3 reps holding stretches for 60 seconds.

Specificity for flexibility:

- ROM is joint specific.

5. **Body Composition:**

Overloading to improve body composition:

- Frequency: daily aerobic exercise,

- Intensity: low;

- Time: approximately one hour.

Progression to improve body composition:

- Begin daily,

- Begin a low aerobic intensity and work up to a longer duration (see cardiorespiratory progression);

- Begin low intensity aerobic exercise for 30 minutes and work up to 60 minutes.

Specificity to improve body composition:

- Increase aerobic exercise and decrease caloric intake.

19.5   Identify the techniques and benefits of warming up and cooling down.

Warming up is a gradual 5 to 10 minute aerobic warm-up utilizing the muscles that will be used in the activity to follow (similar movements at a lower activity). Include stretching of major muscle groups after the gradual warm-up.

The benefits of warming up are:

- Preparing the body for physical activity.

- Reducing the risk of musculoskeletal injuries.

- Releasing oxygen from myoglobin.

- Warming the body's inner core.

- Increasing the reaction of muscles.

- Bringing the heart rate to an aerobic conditioning level.

Cooling down is, basically, the same as warming up - a moderate to light tapering-off of vigorous activity at the end of an exercise session.

The benefits of cooling down are:

- Redistributing circulation of the blood throughout the body to prevent pooling of blood.

- Preventing dizziness.

- Facilitating the removal of lactic acid.

Bibliography

Corbin, Charles B., and Ruth Lindsey. *Concepts of Physical Fitness.* 8th ed. Dubuque, IA: Wm. C. Brown, 1994.

Donatelle, Rebecca, Christine Snow-Harter, and Anthony Wilcox. *Wellness Choices for Health and Fitness.* Redwood City, CA: The Benjamin/Cummings Publishing Company, Inc., 1995.

Heyward, Vivian H. *Designs for Fitness.* Minneapolis: Burgess Publishing Company, 1984.

Insel, Paul M., and Walton T. Roth. *Core Concepts in Health.* 7th ed. Mountain View, CA: Mayfield Publishing Company, 1996 Update.

Kusenitz, Ivan, and Morton Fine. *Your Guide To Getting Fit.* Mountain View, CA: Mayfield Publishing Company, 1987.

Lindsey, Ruth, Billie J. Jones, and Ada Van Whitley. *Fitness for the Health of It.* 6th ed. Dubuque, IA: Wm. C. Brown, 1989.

McArdle, William D., Frank I. Katch, and Victor L. Katch. *Exercise Physiology: Energy, Nutrition, and Human Performance.* 2nd ed. Philadelphia: Lea & Febiger, 1986.

Rosato, Frank D. *Fitness for Wellness: The Physical Connection.* 3rd ed. Minneapolis/St. Paul: West Publishing Company.

Stokes, Roberta, and Clancy. Moore. *Personal Fitness and You.* 3rd ed. Winston-Salem, NC: Hunter, 1993.

Williams, Charles, Emmanouel G. Harageones, DeWayne J. Johnson, and Charles D. Smith. *Personal Fitness: Looking Good/Feeling Good.* Dubuque, IA: Kendall/Hunt, 1984.

20.0   Knowledge of fitness value of activities.

    20.1   **Identify the health- and skill-related components of physical fitness developed by selected activities.**

1. Aerobic Dance:
    Health related components of fitness = *cardiorespiratory; controls body composition.*
    Skill related components of fitness = *agility; coordination.*

2. Bicycling:
    Health related components of fitness = *cardiorespiratory, muscle strength, muscle endurance; controls body composition.*
    Skill related components of fitness = *balance.*

3. Calisthenics:
    Health related components of fitness = *cardiorespiratory, muscle strength, muscle endurance, flexibility; controls body fat.*
    Skill related components of fitness = *agility.*

4. Circuit Training:
    Health related components of fitness = *cardiorespiratory, muscle strength, muscle endurance; controls body composition.*
    Skill related components of fitness = *power.*

5. Cross Country Skiing:
    Health related component of fitness = *cardiorespiratory, muscle strength, muscle endurance; controls body composition.*
    Skill related components of fitness = *agility, coordination; power.*

6. Jogging/Running:
    Health related components of fitness = *cardiorespiratory; controls body fat.*

7. Rope Jumping:
    Health related components of fitness = *cardiorespiratory; controls body composition.*
    Skill related components of fitness = *agility, coordination, reaction time; speed.*

8. Rowing:
    Health related components of fitness = *cardiorespiratory, muscle strength, muscle endurance; controls body composition.*
    Skill related components of fitness = *agility, coordination; power.*

9. Skating:
    Health related components of fitness = *cardiorespiratory; controls body composition.*
    Skill related components of fitness = *agility, balance, coordination; speed.*

10. Swimming/Water Exercises:
    Health related components of fitness = *cardiorespiratory, muscle strength, muscle endurance, flexibility; controls body composition.*
    Skill related components of fitness = *agility; coordination.*

80

11. Walking (brisk):
    Health related components of fitness = *cardiorespiratory; controls body composition.*

Bibliography

Corbin, Charles B., and Ruth Lindsey. *Concepts of Physical Fitness.* 8th ed. Dubuque, IA: Wm. C. Brown. 1994.

Donatelle, Rebecca J., Christine Snow-Harter, and Anthony Wilcox. *Wellness Choices for Health and Fitness.* Redwood City, CA: The Benjamin/Cummings Publishing Company, Inc., 1995.

Stokes, Roberta and Clancy Moore. *Personal Fitness and You.* 3rd ed. Winston-Salem, NC: Hunter, 1993.

Williams, Charles, Emmanouel G. Harageones, DeWayne J. Johnson, and Charles D. Smith. *Personal Fitness: Looking Good/Feeling Good.* Dubuque, IA: Kendall/Hunt, 1984.

21.0 Knowledge of physical fitness program development.

21.1 Interpret data from fitness assessments.

Data from physical fitness assessments can diagnose an individual's level of fitness and identify the components of fitness requiring improvement. Data are compared to norms.

Cardiorespiratory data identifies an individual's functional aerobic capacity by the predicted maximum oxygen consumption. This can, partially, explain natural leanness, running ability, and motivation.

Muscle strength data identifies an individual's ability to execute some basic skills, an individual's potential of injury, an individual's potential to develop musculoskeletal problems, and an individual's potential to cope with life threatening situations.

Muscle strength data identifies an individual's ability to exercise, continually, for an extended period of time and an individual's potential to develop musculosketetal problems.

Flexibility data identifies an individual's potential of motor skill performance, an individual's potential of developing musculoskeletal problems (including poor posture), and an individual's potential of performing activities of daily living.

Body composition data can be used as an indicator of an individual's health status and an indicator of an individual's potential to participate in physical activities.

21.2 Design physical fitness programs incorporating the health-related components to meet the needs of students.

Fitness programs are designed incorporating: mode, frequency, intensity, and time; progression.

A **cardiorespiratory fitness** program is designed by:

- *Mode:* aerobic activities (i.e. walking, jogging, swimming, cycling, rowing).

- *Frequency:* 3 to 5 days/week.

- *Intensity:* 60% to 90% of maximum oxygen uptake or 60% to 80% THR.

- *Time:* 20 to 60 minutes of continuous or interval (non-continuous) activity [time is dependent on intensity level].

- *Progression:* prescription is adjusted according to an individual's fitness level and conditioning effects.

A **muscle strength** program is designed by:

- *Mode:* weight training (isotonic/dynamic).

- *Frequency:* minimum 3 days/week to a maximum of every other day.

- *Intensity:* 60% to 90% of maximum muscle strength (1-RM).

- *Time:* 3 sets with 3 to 8 reps and a 60 second rest interval.

- *Progression:* increase workload (overload) when individual can perform 15 reps at 10 RM level.

A **muscle endurance** program is designed by:

- *Mode:* weight training.

- *Frequency:* minimum 3 days/week up to every other day.

- *Intensity:* 30% to 60% of maximum muscle strength (1-RM).

- *Time:* 3 sets with 12 to 20 reps or until point of muscle fatigue with a 15 to 60 second rest interval.

- *Progression:* increase workload (overload) periodically based on number of continuous repetitions.

A **flexibility** program is designed by:

- *Mode:* stretching.

- *Frequency:* 3 to 7 days/week.

- *Intensity:* just below individual's threshold of pain.

- *Time:* 3 sets with 3 reps holding stretches 15 to 30 seconds with a 60 rest interval between sets.

A **body composition** program is designed by:

- *Mode:* combining aerobic exercise and weight training and a moderate reduction of caloric intake.

- *Frequency:* minimum of 3 days/week; however, daily is best.

- *Intensity:* low intensity; long duration.

- *Time:* 45 to 60 minutes of aerobic activity; 3 sets with a minimum of 6 reps for weights every other day.

- *Progression:* periodically increase as individual improves.

21.3   **Evaluate personal fitness programs and recommend changes where needed.**

After assessing an individual's fitness level, a personal fitness program can be prescribed. Prescription of a fitness program begins with:

1. Identifying the components of fitness that need changing (via assessment).

2. Establishing short-term goals.

3. Developing a plan to meet the established goals.

4. Keeping records to record progress.

5. Evaluating progress of goals and making changes based on success or failure.

For a successful program, **formulating new goals changes the personal fitness program to accomplish those new goal.**

For unsuccessful programs, **changing the goals, particularly if the goals were too unrealistic, would be appropriate for the individual to make progress and succeed. In addition, analyzing positive and negative reinforcers may identify barriers/obstacles (i.e. personal, environmental, cultural, and group factors [such as family, health personnel, and the media]) that prevent an individual's success in his/her personal fitness program.** Incorporating periodic, positive rewards for advancing can provide positive reinforcement and encouragement.

21.4   **Identify the relationship of body type to body composition and motor performance.**

The **ectomorph** body type is **lean** and is more capable of **motor performance that involves endurance.**

The **mesomorph** body type is **muscular** and more capable of **motor performance that involves strength and power.**

The **endomorph** body type is overfat/obese and **motor performance is poor.**

Bibliography

American Alliance for Health, Physical Education, Recreation and Dance. *Health Related Physical Fitness Test Manual.* Reston, VA: American Alliance for Health, Physical Education, Recreation and Dance, 1980.

Clarke, H. Harrison, and David H. Clarke. *Application of Measurement to Physical Education.* 6th ed. Englewood Cliffs, NJ: Prentice-Hall, 1987.

Corbin, Charles B., and Ruth Lindsey. *Concepts of Physical Fitness.* 8th ed. Dubuque, IA: Wm. C. Brown.

Donatelle, Rebecca J., and Lorraine G. Davis. *Access to Health.* 4th ed. Boston: Allyn and Bacon, 1996.

Heyward, Vivian H. *Designs for Fitness.* Minneapolis: Burgess Publishing Company, 1984.

Katch, Frank, and William D. McArdle. *Nutrition, Weight Control and Exercise.* 2nd ed. Philadelphia: Lea & Febiger, 1983.

Kirkendall, Don R., Joseph J. Gruber, and Robert E. Johnson. *Measurement and Evaluation for Physical Educators.* 2nd ed. Champaign, IL: Human Kinetics, 1987.

Lindsey, Ruth, Billie J. Jones, and Ada Van Whitley. *Fitness for the Health of It.* 6th ed. Dubuque. IA: Wm. C. Brown, 1989.

Maud, Peter J., and Carl Foster (Eds.). *Physiological Assessment of Human Fitness.* Champaign, IL: Human Kinetics, 1995.

McArdle, William D., Frank I. Katch, and Victor L. Katch. *Essentials of Exercise Physiology.* Philadelphia: Lea & Febiger, 1994.

McArdle, William D., Frank I. Katch, and Victor L. Katch. *Exercise Physiology: Energy, Nutrition, and Human Performance.* 2nd ed. Philadelphia: Lea & Febiger, 1986.

Safrit, Margret J., and Terry M. Wood. *Introduction to Measurement in Physical Education and Exercise Science.* 3rd ed. St. Louis: Times Mirror/Mosby, 1995.

Stokes, Roberta, and Clancy. Moore. *Personal Fitness and You.* 3rd ed. Winston-Salem, NC: Hunter, 1993.

Williams, Charles, Emmanouel G. Harageones, DeWayne J. Johnson, and Charles D. Smith. *Personal Fitness: Looking Good/Feeling Good.* Dubuque, IA: Kendall/Hunt, 1984.

22.0 Knowledge of effects of exercise and healthful living on stress.

22.1 Identify common signs of stress.

Emotional signs of stress include: depression, lethargy, aggressiveness, irritability, anxiety, edginess, fearfulness, impulsiveness, chronic fatigue hyperexcitability, inability to concentrate, frequent feelings of boredom, feeling overwhelmed, apathy, impatience, pessimism, sarcasm, humorlessness, confusion, helplessness, melancholy, alienation, purposelessness, isolation, numbness, self-consciousness; inability to maintain an intimate relationship.

Behavioral signs of stress include: elevated use of substances (alcohol, drugs; tobacco), crying, yelling, insomnia or excessive sleep, excessive TV watching, school/job burnout, panic attacks, poor problem solving capability, avoidance of people, aberrant behavior, procrastination, accident proneness, restlessness, loss of memory, indecisiveness, aggressiveness, inflexibility, phobic responses, tardiness, disorganization; sexual problems.

Physical signs of stress: pounding heart, stuttering, trembling/nervous tics, excessive perspiration, teeth grinding, gastrointestinal problems (constipation, indigestion, diarrhea, queasy stomach), dry mouth, aching lower back, migraine/tension headaches, stiff neck, asthma attacks, allergy attacks, skin problems, frequent colds or low grade fevers, muscle tension, hyperventilation, high blood pressure, amenorrhea, nightmares; cold intolerance.

22.2 Identify common "stressors" which may affect individuals.

Individuals are affected by the following common stressors: death of a spouse, death of a close family member or a close personal friend, divorce or separation from a significant other, divorce of parents, addition of a new family member, personal injury/illness, unintentional pregnancy, getting married, jail term, dysfunctional family and social ties, financial problems, fired from a job, moving, poor time management, overcrowding, expectations of others, workaholic personality, lack of self-control and self confidence and self-efficacy, low self-esteem, lack of social support, general insecurity, change, heat/cold extremes, poor living conditions, unsafe work environment, one's occupation, retirement, academic/business readjustment, taking out a major loan, discrimination, being a victim of a crime, exposure to water borne or air borne chemicals; noise.

22.3 Identify both positive and negative coping strategies for individuals under stress.

Positive coping strategies to cope with stress include: using one's social support system, spiritual support, managing time, initiating direct action, re-examining priorities, active thinking, acceptance, meditation, imagery, biofeedback, progressive relaxation, deep breathing, massage, sauna, jacuzzi, humor, recreation and diversions, and exercise.

Negative coping strategies to cope with stress include: using alcohol or other mind altering substances, smoking, excessive caffeine intake, poor eating habits, negative "self-talk;" expressing feelings of distress, anger, and other feelings in a destructive manner.

Bibliography

Corbin, Charles B., and Ruth Lindsey. *Concepts of Physical Fitness.* 8th ed. Dubuque, IA: Wm. C. Brown, 1994.

Donatelle, Rebecca, and Lorraine G. Davis. *Access to Health.* 4th ed. Boston: Allyn and Bacon, 1996.

Donatelle, Rebecca J., Christine Snow-Harter, and Anthony Wilcox. *Wellness Choices for Health and Fitness.* Redwood City, CA: The Benjamin/Cummings Publishing Company, Inc., 1995.

Insel, Paul M., and Walton T. Roth. *Core Concepts in Health.* 7th ed. Mountain View, CA: Mayfield Publishing Company, 1996 Update.

Rosato, Frank D. *Fitness for Wellness: The Physical Connection.* 3rd ed. Minneapolis/St. Paul: West Publishing Company, 1994.

Stokes, Roberta, and Clancy Moore. *Personal Fitness and You.* 3rd ed. Winston-Salem, NC: Hunter, 1993.

Williams, Charles, Emmanouel G. Harageones, DeWayne J. Johnson, and Charles D. Smith. *Personal Fitness: Looking Good/Feeling Good.* Dubuque, IA: Kendall/Hunt, 1984.

23.0   Knowledge of nutrition and weight control.

23.1   Identify the components of nutrition.

The components of nutrition are *carbohydrates, proteins, fats, vitamins, minerals, and water.*

Carbohydrates are organic compounds organized with a ratio of one atom of carbon and two atoms of hydrogen for each oxygen atom. Carbohydrates are classified as simple or complex. **Simple carbohydrates** include **monosaccharides** (glucose, fructose, and galactose which contain only one molecule of sugar) and **disaccharides** (sucrose, maltose, and lactose which have a 1:2 ratio). **Complex carbohydrates** (polysaccharides which have a 1:3 ratio) include **starches** (seeds, corn, various grains that make up pastas, breads, cereals, green leafy vegetables, cruciferous vegetables, yellow fruits and vegetables, and certain root vegetables) and **fiber.** Fiber is **insoluble** (increases bulk in stool and softens stool by absorbing water) or **soluble** (slows glucose absorption and may lower cholesterol levels).

Proteins are organic substances composed of carbon, hydrogen, oxygen, and nitrogen. Proteins are mainly responsible for the maintenance/growth and repair of body tissue. Proteins are either **complete** or **incomplete.** Complete proteins are found in foods from animal tissue and **supply all essential amino acids.** Incomplete proteins are found in complex carbohydrates and are **deficient in one or two essential amino acids.** Incomplete proteins can be complete proteins by either complementing or supplementing (eating two incomplete proteins in the same meal).

Fats (lipids) are organic substances consisting of carbon, hydrogen, and oxygen. Fats have a high oxygen-hydrogen ratio (1:7). Fats are either **saturated** or **unsaturated.** **Saturated fats** are chains of fatty acids that are **incapable of holding any more hydrogen** (the fatty acid chain is filled to capacity). Saturated fats are solid at room temperature and, generally, come from animal sources.

The two types of unsaturated fats, **monounsaturated and polyunsaturated,** have room for additional hydrogen atoms in their chemical structure; therefore, **the number of hydrogen atoms that are missing is applicable to the terms monounsaturated and polyunsaturated.** Monounsaturated fats **have room for one hydrogen-binding site** in the fatty acid's double-bond carbon chain (one hydrogen bond is missing). Polyunsaturated fats have **room for two or more hydrogen binding sites** in the fatty acid's double-bond carbon chain (two or more hydrogen bonds are missing). Unsaturated fats, generally, are liquid at room temperature and come from plants (including vegetable oils).

Vitamins are organic compounds, each having a specific function. Vitamins do not supply energy; however, their most important role is acting as catalysts to facilitate the processing of carbohydrates, proteins, and fats from food - transforming them into energy and regulating metabolic functions.

Vitamins are classified as **fat-soluble or water-soluble.** Fat-soluble vitamins (A, D, E, and K) are stored in the body for relatively long periods of time and are toxic if consistently taken in large amounts. Water-soluble vitamins perform a fundamental role as part of coenzymes in the intricate series of energy-generating reactions occurring within the body's cells. Water-soluble vitamins (the B vitamins and C) remain in the body for a short time; thus, they need to be consumed on a regular basis.

Minerals are inorganic compounds (do not contain carbon) required in small amounts to regulate body processes and maintain internal processes. Minerals are important for enzyme synthesis, basic bone and teeth formation, normal digestion functioning, and the regulation of the heart muscle. Regular over-consumption of minerals can produce an excess accumulation in the body leading to toxicity.

Water is the most essential nutrient of all without which one can only live for approximately three days. Water constitutes about 50% - 55% of a woman's body and about 55% - 60% of a man's body. Body water performs three essential functions for life: 1) the mode for sustaining a stable body temperature, 2) providing the necessary chemical solvent in which the immense variety of body tissue solutions are based, and 3) furnishing a "fullness" to body tissues vital for body form.

23.2   Determine the adequacy of diets in meeting the nutritional needs of students.

Nutritional requirements *vary from person-to-person.* General guidelines for meeting adequate nutritional needs are as follows: *no more than 30% total caloric intake from fats* (preferably 10% from saturated fats, 10% from monounsaturated fats; 10% from polyunsaturated fats), *no more than 15% total caloric intake from protein* (complete), *and at least 55% of caloric intake from carbohydrates* (mainly complex carbohydrates).

23.4   Determine the role of exercise and diet in the maintenance of proper weight management.

Exercise and diet maintains proper body weight by equalizing caloric intake to caloric output achieved by a permanent change in behavior. An individually, tailored food plan, that is well-balanced, combined with a personalized exercise program, that is well designed is effective and personally rewarding. Generally, weight management is based on a person's detailed weight history. In addition, determining energy balance levels, individual weight needs and problems, and personal living situations must be assessed.

An individual program must meet needs and goals. Some form of the following elements should be included:

1. *Food Behaviors* - Recording the amount of food served and consumed, noting the time it takes to consume food, becoming aware of hidden fat, sugar, and salt to reduce their intake, increasing fiber consumption, choosing a variety of foods that are nutrient dense and lower in fat and caloric content; reducing consumption of processed foods.

2. *Exercise Behaviors* - Scheduling daily exercise that includes a form of aerobic exercise, setting periodic goals, and keeping progress records.

3. *Stress Reduction Exercises* - Scheduling and practicing exercises that reduce stress such as meditation, progressive muscle relaxation, or imagery.

4. *Personal Interest Area* - Forming new activities that do not center around food, such as intellectual stimulation. Exploring community resources can provide avenues to participate in diverting, interesting, and enjoyable activities.

5. *Follow-Up Program* - Scheduling appointments with a nutritionist can provide exploration of problems, anticipate needs, avoid set-backs, and review progress. Moreover, support and encouragement can be provided as well as motivation to maintain a program.

23.5   Recognize fallacies and dangers underlying selected diet plans.

High Carbohydrate diets (i.e. Pritikin; Bloomingdale's) can produce rapid or gradual weight loss, depending on caloric intake. Vitamin and mineral supplements are usually recommended because protein intake is low - which can be difficult to maintain. These diets may/may not recommend exercising or permanent lifestyle changes which are necessary to maintain one's weight.

High Protein Diets, basically, have the same myths, fallacies, and results as high carbohydrate diets. High protein diets also require vitamin and mineral supplements. In addition, these diets are usually high in saturated fats and cholesterol because of the emphasis on protein which, naturally, are found in meat products.

Liquid Formulas that are physician/hospital run (i.e. Medifast; Optifast) provide 800 or less calories a day that are consumed in liquid form. Dieters forgo food intake for 12 to 16 weeks in lieu of the protein supplement. Vitamin and mineral supplements and close medical supervision are required. Food is gradually reintroduced after the initial fast. These diets can result in severe and/or dangerous metabolic problems in addition to an irregular heartbeat, kidney infections and failure, hair loss, and sensation of feeling cold and/or cold intolerance. These are very expensive and have a high rate of failure.

Over-The-Counter Liquid Diets (i.e. Slimfast) are liquid/food bar supplements are taken in place of one or more meals per day and advocate an intake of 1,000 calories daily. Carbohydrates, protein, vitamins, and minerals may be so low that they can be as dangerous as the medically supervised liquid diets when relied on for the only source of nutrition. Because of no medical supervision, the side-effects can be even more dangerous.

Over-The-Counter Diet Pills/Aids and Prescription Diet Pills (appetite suppressants) have as their main ingredient phenyl propanolamine hydrochloride [PPA], which has reported, contradictory, effectiveness. Keeping weight off by the use of these products is difficult. Dizziness, sleeplessness, high blood pressure, palpitation, headaches, and tachycardia have been reported with the use of these products. Moreover, prescription diet pills can be addictive.

Low Calorie Diets (caloric restricted) are the most misunderstood way individuals lose weight; however, restricting the intake of calories is the way most people choose to lose weight. All the focus is on food creating anxiety over the restriction of food - especially favorite foods. These diets are also difficult to maintain and have a high failure rate. Like the other diets, once the diet is over, weight is regained because of not making permanent behavior changes. Side-effects of caloric restriction include: diarrhea, constipation, Ketosis, a lower basal metabolic rate, blood sugar imbalances, loss of lean body tissue, fatigue, weakness, and emotional problems. Dietary supplements are needed.

Those who choose *Fasting* to lose weight can deplete enough of the body's energy stores that the result can be death.

Bibliography

Corbin, Charles B., and Ruth Lindsey. *Concepts of Physical Fitness.* 8th ed. Dubuque, IA: Wm. C. Brown, 1994.

Donatelle, Rebecca J., and Lorraine G. Davis. *Access to Health.* 4th ed. Boston: Allyn and Bacon, 1996.

Donatelle, Rebecca, Christine Snow-Harter, and Anthony Wilcox. *Wellness Choices for Health and Fitness.* Redwood City, CA: The Benjamin/Cummings Publishing Company, Inc., 1995.

Insel, Paul. M., and Walton T. Roth. *Core Concepts in Health.* 7th ed. Mountain View, CA: Mayfield Publishing Company, 1996 Update.

Katch, Frank, and McArdle, William D. *Nutrition, Weight Control, and Exercise.* 2nd ed. Philadelphia: Lea & Febiger.

McArdle, William D., Frank I. Katch, and Victor L. Katch. *Essentials of Exercise Physiology.* Philadelphia: Lea & Febiger, 1994.

McArdle, William D., Frank I. Katch, and Victor L. Katch. *Exercise Physiology: Energy Nutrition, and Human Performance.* 2nd ed. Philadelphia: Lea & Febiger, 1986.

Miller, D, and T. E. Miller. *Fitness: A Life-Time Commitment.* 3rd ed. Edina, MN: Burgess, 1986.

Rosato, Frank D. *Fitness for Wellness: The Physical Connection.* 3rd ed. Minneapolis/St. Paul: West Publishing Company, 1994.

Stokes, R., and C. Moore. *Personal Fitness and You.* Winston-Salem, NC: Hunter, 1986.

University of California, Berkeley. *The Wellness Encyclopedia.* Boston: Houghton Mifflin Company.

Williams, Sue Rodwell. *Nutrition and Diet Therapy.* 7th ed. St. Louis: Mosbey.

Williams, Charles, Emmanouel G. Harageones, DeWayne J. Johnson, and Charles D. Smith. *Personal Fitness: Looking Good/Feeling Good.* Dubuque, IA: Kendall/Hunt, 1984.

Williams, Melvin. *Nutrition for Fitness and Sport.* Dubuque, IA: Brown, 1983.

24.0 Knowledge of health risk factors.

24.1 Identify health risk factors which can be improved by engaging in physical activity.

The following risk factors may be improved by physical activity: cholesterol levels, blood pressure, stress related disorders, heart diseases, overfatness and obesity disorders, early death, certain types of cancer , musculoskeletal problems, mental health, and susceptibility to infectious diseases.

Bibliography

Corbin, Charles B., and Ruth Lindsey. *Concepts of Physical Fitness.* 8th ed. Dubuque, IA: Wm. C. Brown, 1994.

Donatelle, Rebecca J., and Lorraine G. Davis. *Access to Health.* 4th ed. Boston: Allyn and Bacon, 1996.

Donatelle, Rebecca, Christine Snow-Harter, and Anthony Wilcox. *Wellness Choices for Health and Fitness.* Redwood City, CA: The Benjamin/Cummings Publishing Company, 1995.

Stokes, Roberta, and Clancy Moore. *Personal Fitness and You.* 3rd ed. Winston-Salem, NC: Hunter, 1993.

Williams, Charles, Emmanouel G. Harageones, DeWayne J. Johnson, and Charles D. Smith. *Personal Fitness: Looking Good/Feeling Good.* Dubuque, IA: Kendall/Hunt, 1984.

92

25.0 Knowledge of the benefits of exercise.

25.1 Identify the physiological, psychological, and sociological benefits of physical activity.

Physiological benefits of physical activity include the following: improved cardiorespiratory fitness, improved muscle strength, improved muscle endurance, improved flexibility, more lean muscle mass and less body fat, quicker recovery rate, improves the body's ability to utilize oxygen, lowers the resting heart rate, increases cardiac output, improves venous return and peripheral circulation, reduces the risk of musculoskeletal injuries, improves bone mass, cardiac hypertrophy, size and strength of blood vessels, increases the number red cells, improves blood-sugar regulation, improves efficiency of thyroid gland, improves energy regulation, and increases life expectancy.

Psychological benefits of physical activity include the following: relieves stress, improved mental health via better physical health, reduces mental tension (relieves depression, improves sleeping patterns; less stress symptoms), better resistance to fatigue, better quality of life, more enjoyment of leisure, better capability to handle some stressors, opportunity of successful experiences, better Self-Concept, better ability to recognize and accept limitations, improved appearance and sense of well-being, better ability to meet challenges, and better sense of accomplishments.

Sociological benefits of physical activity include: the opportunity to spend time with family and friends, making new friends, the opportunity to be part of a team, the opportunity to participate in competitive experiences; the opportunity to experience the thrill of victories.

25.2 Identify exercises that benefit the major muscle groups of the body.

Major muscle groups of the body benefited by exercise are: trapezius, deltoids, pectorals, latissimus dorsi, obliques, abdominals, biceps, triceps, quadriceps, hamstrings, abductors and adductors, calves, and gluteus (maximus, medius, and minimus).

Exercises benefiting the **trapezius** include: dumbbell shoulder shrug, barbell shoulder shrug, and universal machine shoulder shrug.

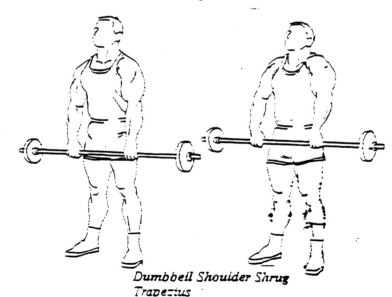

Dumbbell Shoulder Shrug
Trapezius

Exercises benefiting the **deltoids** include: incline bench press, military press, behind-the-neck press, power clean, dumbbell press (upright and incline press), and rows (upright and bent-over).

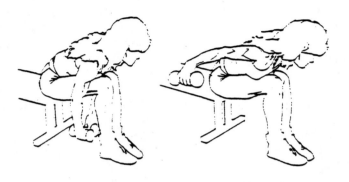

Seated Bent-Over Rear Deltoid Raise
Rear Deltoids

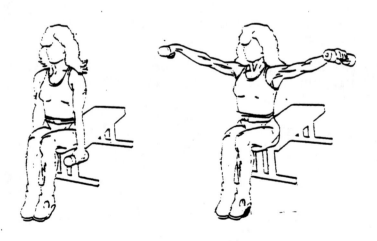

Seated Side Lateral Raise
Front and Outer Deltoids

Exercises benefiting the **pectorals** include: barbell bench press (close-grip. medium-grip; wide-grip), incline barbell press. decline barbell press, incline dumbbell press. decline dumbbell press, dumbbell flyes. baarbell pullovers, dumbbell pullovers. and pushups.

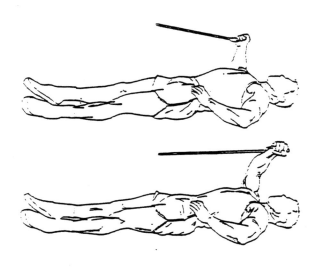

Lying Low-Pulley One-Arm Chest Lateral
Pectorals

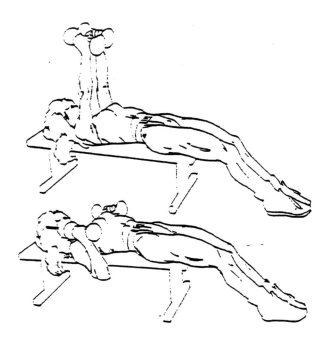

Flat Dumbbell Press
Pectorals

Exercises benefiting the **latissimus dorsi** include: lat pull-downs - front, lat pull-downs - back., bent-over dumbbell rowing, one-arm long bar rowing, two-arm long bar rowing, and barbell rowing.

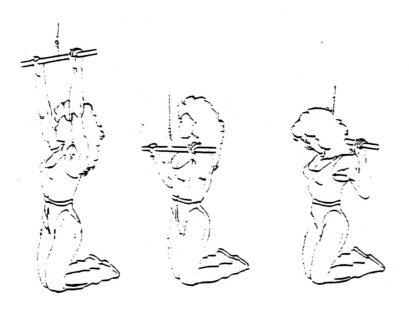

Medium-Grip Front-to-Rear Lat Pull-Down
Lats

Straight-Arm Close-Grip Lat Pulldown
Lats

Exercises benefiting the **obliques** include: barbell side bends, dumbbell side bends, stiff-legged dumbbell dead lift, stiff-legged barbell dead lift, dumbbell bend to opposite foot, and seated barbell twist.

Dumbbell Side Bend
Obliques

Seated Barbell Twist
Obliques

Exercises benefiting the **abdominals** include: bent-knee situps, leg raises, weighted leg raises, jackknife situps, leg pull-ins, and abdominal crunches.

Leg Pull-In
Lower Abdominals

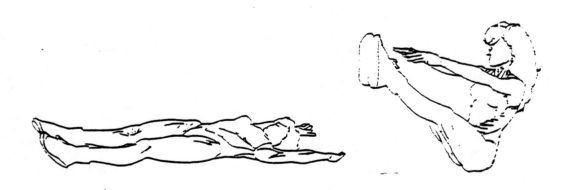

Jackknife Sit-Up
Upper and Lower Abdominals

Exercises benefiting the **biceps** include: dumbbell curls (synchronized, all positions), barbell curls (all positions), scott bench curls (barbell; dumbbell), preacher bench curls (barbell; dumbbell), and pulley curls (synchronized alternate).

Standing Alternated Dumbbell Curl
Biceps

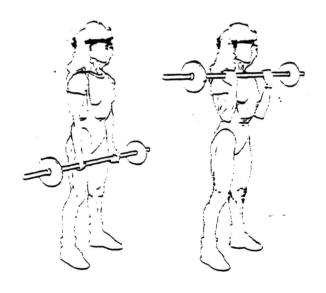

Standing Medium-Grip Barbell Curl
Biceps

Exercises benefiting the **triceps** include: dumbbell overhead curls (standing, sitting; bench), standing bent-over dumbbell extensions (one-arm; two-arm), barbell triceps curls (overhead), standing triceps press-downs, triceps curls (low pulley; high pulley), bench press, incline press, and pushups.

Standing Close-Grip Easy-Curl-Bar Triceps Curl
Triceps

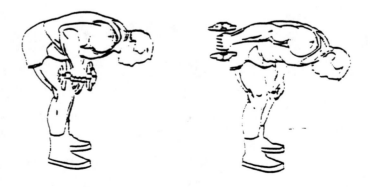

Standing Bent-Over One-Arm-Dumbbell Triceps Extension
Triceps

Exercises benefiting the **quadriceps** include: squats/half-squats (all positions), Jefferson lift, front lunges (with/without weights), side lunges (with/without weights), leg extensions (single/double leg on leg extension machine), thrusts (machine thrusts), leg presses (leg press machine), step-ups (with/without weights), and jump squats (with/without weights).

Flat-Footed Medium-Stance Barbell Half-Squat
Thighs

Freehand Front Lunge
Thighs and Hamstrings

Exercises benefiting the **hamstrings** include: front lunges (with/without weights), side lunges (with/without weights), hamstring curls (single/double on leg extension machine), and back extension on waist-high bench.

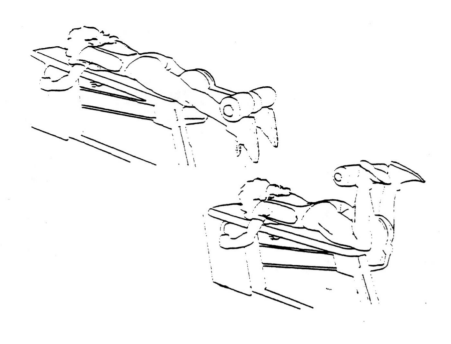

Thigh Biceps Curl on Leg Extension Machine
Hamstrings

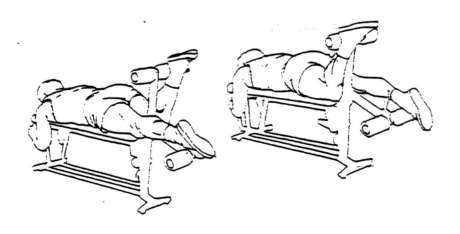

One-at-a-Time Biceps Curl on Leg Extension Machine
Hamstrings

Exercises benefiting the **abductors and adductors** include: side lunges (with/without weights), wide-stance leg press (leg press machine), wide-stance half-squat (thrust machine), leg abductions (with/without resistance), leg crossovers (with/without resistance), abduction against resistance (abductor/adductor machine), and adduction against resistance (abductor/adductor machine).

Hip Abduction
Hips

Hip Adduction
Inner Thigh

Exercises benefiting the **calves** (triceps surae) include: standing toe raises (with/without weights, jump squats (with/without weights), and calf raises (single/double leg on calf raise machine).

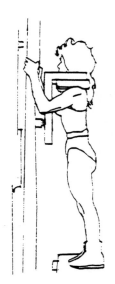

Standing Toe Raise on Wall Calf Machine
Main Calf Muscles

Standing Barbell Toe Raise
Main Calf Muscles

Exercises benefiting the **gluteus** (maximus, medius; minimus) include: leg curls (single/double on leg extension machine), hip extensions (with/without resistance - wall pulley on ankle), and hip flexions (with/without resistance - wall pulley on ankle).

Hip Extension
Hips and Thighs

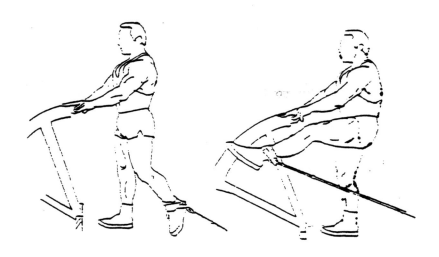

Hip Flexion
Hip Flexors

25.3 **Identify diseases and conditions caused in part by a lack of physical activity.**

Hypertension, atherosclerosis, arteriosclerosis, heart attack, stroke, congestive heart failure, angina, osteoporosis, osteoarthritis, adult on-set diabetes, gout, gall bladder disorders, ulcers, osteoporosis, cancer, lordosis, poor posture, neck, leg, knee, and foot problems are all diseases and conditions caused in part by a lack of physical activity.

Bibliography

Corbin, Charles B., and Ruth Lindsey. *Concepts of Physical Fitness.* 8th ed. Dubuque, IA: Wm. C. Brown, 1994.

Donatelle, Rebecca J., and Lorraine G. Davis. *Access to Health.* 4th ed. Boston: Allyn and Bacon, 1996.

Insel, Paul M., and Walton T. Roth. *Core Concepts in Health.* 7th ed. Mountain View, CA: Mayfield Publishing Company, 1996 Update.

Kusinitz, Ivan and Morton Fine. *Your Guide To Getting Fit.* Palo Alto, CA: Mayfield Publishing Company.

Lindsey, Ruth, Billie J. Jones, and Ada Van Whitley. *Fitness for the Health of It.* 6th ed. Dubuque, IA: Wm. C. Brown, 1989.

Pearl, Bill and Gary T. Moran. *Getting Stronger.* Bolinas, CA: Shelter Publications, Inc., 1986.

Rosato, Frank D. *Fitness for Wellness: The Physical Connection.* 3rd ed. Minneapolis/St. Paul: West Publishing Company, 1994.

Stokes, Roberta, and Clancy. Moore. *Personal Fitness and You.* 3rd ed. Winston-Salem, NC: Prentice-Hall, 1993.

Williams, Charles, Emmanouel G. Harageones, DeWayne J. Johnson, and Charles D. Smith. *Personal Fitness: Looking Good/Feeling Good.* Dubuque, IA: Kendall/Hunt, 1984.

26.0 Knowledge of physical fitness issues related to consumers.

26.1 Identify exercise myths and gimmicks.

Exercise myths and gimmicks include:

- Drinking beer/alcoholic beverages is a good way to replenish loss of body fluids after exercising.

- Women should not exercise while menstruating or pregnant.

- Physically fit people will not die from heart disease.

- You cannot be too flexible.

- Spot reduction is effective.

- Children are naturally active and do not need to exercise.

- Muscle will turn into fat with the cessation of exercising.

- Fat can turn into muscle.

- Women will develop large muscles by weight training, you should exercise while sick regardless how ill you are.

- Cardiac hypertrophy developed by exercising is harmful to health.

- Exercise increases the appetite.

- Exercise gets rid of sagging skin and wrinkles.

- Yoga is a good way to develop fitness.

- Losing cellulite requires special treatment.

- Body wraps are a good way to lose weight.

26.2 Identify exercise equipment as either sound or unsound using physiological principles.

Rolling machines, vibrating belts, vibrating tables and pillows, massaging devices. electrical muscle stimulators, weighted belts, motor-driven cycles and rowing machines. saunas, and plastic or rubberized sweatsuits and sauna suits are *all ineffective exercise equipment because they produce passive movement* (no voluntary muscle contractions). **Sound exercise equipment produces active movement as a result of a person initiating the movement of the equipment or the person voluntarily producing muscle contractions.**

Bibliography

Corbin. Charles B., and Ruth Lindsey. *Concepts of Physical Fitness.* 8th ed. Dubuque, IA: Wm. C. Brown, 1994.

Lindsey, Ruth, Billie J. Jones, and Ada Van Whitley. *Fitness for the Health of It.* Dubuque, IA: Wm. C. Brown, 1989.

Rosato. Frank D. *Fitness for Wellness: The Physical Connection.* 3rd ed. Minneapolis/St. Paul: West Publishing Company, 1994.

Stokes, Roberta, and Clancy Moore. *Personal Fitness and You.* 3rd ed. Winston-Salem, NC: Hunter, 1993.

Williams, Charles. Emmanouel G. Harageones, DeWayne J. Johnson, and Charles D. Smith. *Personal Fitness: Looking Good/Feeling Good.* Dubuque, IA: Kendall/Hunt, 1984.

1. The Greek's best known early contribution to the profession Physical Education was:

   A. the Pentathlon
   B. the Olympics
   C. the Pankration
   D. Acrobatics

2. A major event in the history of physical education occurred among the Romans. Which of the following was identified by the Romans?

   A. Severe physical training
   B. Harmonious development of the body, mind. and spirit
   C. The worth of physical education was dignified
   D. Physical training only for warriors

3. President Eisenhower was alerted to the poor fitness levels of American youths. How was the poor physical conditioning of youths discovered in the Eisenhower Administration?

   A. By WWII Selective Service Examinations
   B. By organizations promoting physical fitness
   C. By the Federal Security Agency
   D. By the Kraus-Webber Tests

4. In 1956. AAHPER Fitness Conferences established:

   A. The President's Council on Youth Fitness
   B. The President's Citizens' Advisory Committee
   C. The President's Council on Physical Fitness
   D. A and B
   E. All of the above

5. The physical education philosophy that is based on experience is:

   A. Naturalism
   B. Pragmatism
   C. Idealism
   D. Existentialism

6. The modern Physical Education philosophy that combines beliefs from different philosophies is:

   A. Eclectic
   B. Humanistic
   C. Individualism
   D. Realism

7. A Physical Education teachers emphasizes healthy attitudes and habits. His/her classes are conducted so that students acquire, think/analyze, and interpret the knowledge necessary for physical activities. The goals and values utilized and the philosophy applied by this instructor is:

   A. Physical Development Goals and Realism Philosophy
   B. Affective Development Goals and Existentialism
   C. Motor Development Goals and Realism Philosophy
   D. Cognitive Development Goals and Idealism Philosophy

8. Social skills and values developed by activity include all of the following except:

   A. Winning at all costs
   B. Making judgments in groups
   C. Communicating and cooperating
   D. Respecting rules and property

9. Activities that enhance team socialization include all of the following except:

   A. Basketball
   B. Soccer
   C. Golf
   D. Volleyball

10. Through physical activities, John has developed self-discipline, fairness, respect for others, and new friends. John has demonstrated which of the following?

    A. Positive cooperation psycho-social influences
    B. Positive group psycho-social influences
    C. Positive individual psycho-social influences
    D. Positive accomplishment psycho-social influences

11. Which of the following psycho-social influences is not considered negative.

A. Avoidance of problems
B. Adherence to exercise
C. Ego-centeredness
D. Role conflict

12. Which professional organization protects amateur sports from becoming corrupt?

A. AIWA
B. AAHPERD
C. NCAA
D. AAU

13. Which professional organization works with legislatures?

A. AIWA
B. AAHPERD
C. ACSM
D. AAU

14. Research in physical education is published in the following periodicals except the:

A. School PE Update
B. Research Quarterly
C. Journal of Physical Education
D. YMCA Magazine

15. The most effective way to promote the physical education curriculum is to:

A. Relate physical education to higher thought processes
B. Relate physical education to humanitarianism
C. Relate physical education to the total educational process
D. Relate physical education to skills necessary to preserve the natural environment

16. The Affective Domain of physical education contributes to all of the following except:

A. Knowledge of exercise, health, and disease
B. Self-actualization
C. An appreciation of beauty
D. Good sportsmanship

17. A physical education instructor anticipates and prevents potential injuries, watches for hidden injuries, and takes an injury evaluation of the entire class. Which of the following strategies to prevent injuries is the teacher demonstrating?

A. Maintaining hiring standards
B. Proper use of equipment
C. Proper procedures for emergencies
D. Participant screening

18. Which of the following is not a consideration for the selection of a facility?

A. Community involvement
B. Custodial staff
C. Availability to women, minorities, and the handicapped
D. Bond issues

19. Which of the following is not a class management technique?

A. Explaining procedures for roll call, excuses, and tardiness
B. Explaining routines for changing and showering
C. Explaining conditioning
D. Promoting individual self-discipline

20. Long-term planning also is essential for an instructor to manage a class. Identify the management techniques not essential to long-term planning.

A. Parental observation
B. Progress evaluation
C. Precise activity planning
D. Arrangements for line markings

21. Although Mary is a paraplegic, she wants to participate, in some capacity, in the physical education class. What federal legislative act entitles her to do so?

A. PE 94-142
B. Title IX
C. PL 94-142
D. Title XI

22. A legal wrong resulting in a direct or an indirect injury is:

A. Negligence
B. A Tort
C. In loco parentis
D. Legal liability

23. All of the following actions avoid a lawsuit except:

   A. Ensuring equipment and facilities are safe
   B. Getting exculpatory agreements
   C. Knowing each students' health status
   D. Grouping students with unequal competitive levels

24. Which of the following actions does not promote safety?

   A. Allowing students to wear the current style of shoes
   B. Presenting organized activities
   C. Inspecting equipment and facilities
   D. Instructing skill and activities properly

25. An instructor notices that class participation is much lower than expected. By making changes in equipment and rules, the instructor applied which of the following concepts to enhance participation?

   A. Homogeneous grouping
   B. Heterogeneous grouping
   C. Multi-activity designs
   D. Activity modification

26. Using tactual clues is a functional adaptation that can assist with which type of limitation?

   A. Deaf students
   B. Blind students
   C. Asthmatic students
   D. Physically challenged students

27. Which of the following is not a skill assessment test to evaluate student performance?

   A. Harrocks Volley
   B. Rodgers Strength Test
   C. Iowa Brace Test
   D. AAHPERD Youth Fitness Test

28. All of the following are methods to evaluate the Affective Domain except:

   A. Adams Prosocial Inventory
   B. Crowell Personal Distance Scale
   C. Blanchard Behavior Rating Scale
   D. McCloy's Prosocial Behavior Scale

29. The Cognitive Domain can be evaluated by all of the following methods except:

   A. Norm-Referenced Tests
   B. Criterion Referenced Tests
   C. Standardized Tests
   D. Willis Sports Inventory Tests

30. Coordinated movements that springs one over an obstacle is which locomotor skill:

   A. Jumping
   B. Vaulting
   C. Leaping
   D. Hopping

31. Students using the same foot to take off from a surface and land is which locomotor skill?

   A. Jumping
   B. Vaulting
   C. Leaping
   D. Hopping

32. Which nonlocomotor skill entails movement around a joint where two body parts meet?

   A. Twisting
   B. Swaying
   C. Bending
   D. Stretching

33. A sharp change of direction from one's original line of movement is which nonlocomotor skill?

   A. Twisting
   B. Dodging
   C. Swaying
   D. Swinging

34. Which manipulative skill uses the hands to stop the momentum of an object?

   A. Trapping
   B. Catching
   C. Striking
   D. Rolling

35. Playing "Simon Says" and having students touch different body parts applies which movement concept?

    A. Spatial Awareness
    B. Effort Awareness
    C. Body Awareness
    D. Motion Awareness

36. Which movement concept involves students making decisions of an object's positional changes in space?

    A. Spatial Awareness
    B. Effort Awareness
    C. Body Awareness
    D. Motion Awareness

37. Applying the mechanical principles of balance, time, and force is the movement concept of which of the following?

    A. Spatial Awareness
    B. Effort Awareness
    C. Body Awareness
    D. Motion Awareness

38. Having students moving on their hands and knees, moving on lines, and/or holding shapes while moving develops which quality of movement's mechanical principle?

    A. Balance
    B. Time
    C. Force
    D. Inertia

39. Students that paddle balls against a wall or jump over objects with various heights are developing which quality of movement's mechanical principle?

    A. Balance   C. Force
    B. Time   D. Inertia

40. Having students move in a specific pattern while measuring how long they take to do so develops which quality of movement's mechanical principle?

    A. Balance   C. Force
    B. Time   D. Inertia

41. There are two sequential phases to develop spatial awareness. Which is the order of these phases?

    A. Locating more than one object to each object; the location of objects in relation to one's own body in space.
    B. The location of objects in relation to ones' own body in space; locating more than one object in relation to one's own body.
    C. Locating more than one object independent of one's body; the location of objects in relation to one's own body.
    D. The location of objects in relation to one's own body in space; locating more than one object in relation to each object and independent of one's own body.

42. This is an example of which type of lever?

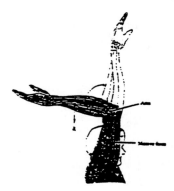

    A. First Class
    B. Second Class
    C. Third Class

43. This is an example of which type of lever?

    A. First Class
    B. Second Class
    C. Third Class

44. This is an example of which type of lever?

A. First Class
B. Second Class
C. Third Class

45. Equilibrium is maintained as long as:

A. Body segments are moved independently.
B. The center of gravity is over the base of support
C. Force is applied to the base of support.
D. The center of gravity is lowered.

46. Which of the following does not enhance equilibrium?

A. Shifting the center of gravity away from the direction of movement.
B. Increasing the base of support.
C. Lowering the base of support.
D. Increasing the base of support and lowering the center of support.

47. Force is affected by the following except:

A. Magnitude
B. Energy
C. Motion
D. Mass

48. For a movement to occur, inertia of an object and any other resisting forces must be overcome by enough force. What concept of force does this describe?

A. Potential energy
B. Magnitude
C. Kinetic energy
D. Absorption

49. The energy of an object to do work while recoiling is which type of potential energy?

A. Absorption
B. Kinetic
C. Elastic
D. Torque

50. Gradually decelerating a moving mass by utilization of smaller forces over a longer period of time is:

A. Stability
B. Equilibrium
C. Angular force
D. Force absorption

51. The tendency of a body/object to remain in its present state of motion unless some force acts to change it is which mechanical principle of motion?

A. Acceleration
B. Inertia
C. Action/Reaction
D. Linear motion

52. The movement response of a system depends not only on how much net external force is applied to it but also on the resistance to movement change is which mechanical principle of motion?

A. Acceleration
B. Inertia
C. Action/Reaction
D. Air Resistance

53. Which of the following mechanical principles of motion states that every motion has a similar, contrasting response?

A. Acceleration
B. Inertia
C. Action/Reaction
D. Centripetal force

54. What is the proper order of sequential development for the acquisition of locomotor skills?

   A. Creep, crawl, walk, jump, run, slide, gallop, hop, leap, skip; step-hop.
   B. Crawl, walk, creep, slide, walk, run, hop, leap, gallop, skip; step-hop.
   C. Creep, crawl, walk, slide, run, hop, leap, skip, gallop, jump; step-hop.
   D. Crawl, creep, walk, run, jump, hop, gallop, slide, leap, skip; step-hop.

55. Having students pretend they are playing basketball or trying to catch a bus develops which locomotor skill?

   A. Galloping
   B. Running
   C. Leaping
   D. Skipping

56. Having students play Fox and Hound is an activity that develops:

   A. Galloping
   B. Hopping
   C. Stepping-hopping
   D. Skipping

57. Having students take off and land while both feet are together develops which locomotor skill?

   A. Hopping
   B. Jumping
   C. Leaping
   D. Skipping

58. What is the proper sequential order of development for the acquisition of locomotor skills?

   A. Stretch, sit, bend, turn, swing, twist, shake, rock & sway, dodge; fall.
   B. Bend, stretch, turn, twist, swing, sit, rock & sway, shake, dodge; fall.
   C. Stretch, bend, sit, shake, turn, rock & sway, swing, twist, dodge; fall.
   D. Bend, stretch, sit, turn, twist, swing, sway, rock & sway, dodge; fall.

59. Activities such as pretending to pick fruit off a tree or reach for a star develops which nonlocomotor skill.

   A. Bending
   B. Stretching
   C. Turning
   D. Twisting

60. Picking up coins, tying shoes, and petting animals develops this nonlocomotor skill.

   A. Bending
   B. Stretching
   C. Turning
   D. Twisting

61. Having students collapse in their own space or lower themselves as though they are a raindrop or snowflake develops this nonlocomotor skill.

   A. Dodging
   B. Shaking
   C. Swinging
   D. Falling

62. Which is the proper sequential order of development for the acquisition of manipulative skills?

   A. Striking, throwing, bouncing, catching, trapping, kicking, ball rolling; volleying.
   B. Striking, throwing, kicking, ball rolling, volleying, bouncing, catching; trapping.
   C. Striking, throwing, catching, trapping, kicking, ball rolling, bouncing; volleying.
   D. Striking, throwing, kicking, ball rolling, bouncing; volleying.

63. Having students hit a large balloon with both hands develops this manipulative skill.

   A. Bouncing
   B. Striking
   C. Volleying
   D. Trapping

64. Progressively decreasing the size of a target that balls are projected at develops which manipulative skill.

A. Throwing
B. Trapping
C. Volleying
D. Kicking

65. Hitting a stationary object while in a fixed position, then incorporating movement, develops this manipulative skill?

A. Bouncing
B. Trapping
C. Throwing
D. Striking

66. A subjective, observational approach to identify errors in the form, style, or mechanics of a skill is accomplished by:

A. Product assessment
B. Process assessment
C. Standardized norm-referenced tests
D. Criterion-referenced tests

67. Fundamental skills can objectively be measured by using this type of assessment?

A. Process assessment
B. Product assessment
C. Texas PE Test
D. Iowa Brace Test

68. Process assessment does not identify which of the following errors in skill performance?

A. Style
B. Form
C. End result
D. Mechanics

69. Determining poor performance of a skill using process assessment can best be accomplished by:

A. Observing how fast a skill is performed.
B. Observing how many skills are performed.
C. Observing how far or how high a skill is performed.
D. Observing several attributes comprising the entire performance of a skill.

70. Which of the following principles is not a factor to assess to correct errors in performance for process assessment?

A. Inertia
B. Action/Reaction
C. Force
D. Acceleration

71. Which of the following ways measures fundamental skills using product assessment?

A. Criterion-referenced tests
B. Standardized norm-referenced tests
C. Both A and B
D. Neither A nor B

72. Product assessment measures all of the following except:

A. How the mechanics of a skill can be performed.
B. How many times a skill can be performed.
C. How fast a skill can be performed.
D. How far or high a skill can be performed.

73. Skill level of achievement in archery can be evaluated by:

A. Giving students a written exam on terminology.
B. Having students demonstrate the correct tension of arrow feathers.
C. Totaling a student's score obtained on the target's face.
D. Time how long a student takes to shoot all arrows.

74. Skill level achievement in golf can be determined by:

    A. The number of "birdies" that were made.
    B. The number of "bogies" that were made.
    C. The score obtained after several rounds.
    D. The total score achieved throughout the school year.

75. Skill level achievement in swimming can be determined by:

    A. How long a student can float.
    B. How many strokes it takes to swim a specified distance.
    C. How long a student can stay under the water without moving.
    D. How many times a student can dive in five minutes.

76. Skill level achievement in bowling can be accomplished by:

    A. Calculating a student's average.
    B. Calculating how many gutter-balls were thrown.
    C. Calculating how many strikes were thrown.
    D. Calculating how many spares were thrown.

77. Although they are still hitting the target, the score of some students practicing archery has lowered when the distance between them and the target has decreased. Which of the following adjustments will improve their scores?

    A. Increasing the velocity of their arrows.
    B. Increasing the students' base of support.
    C. Increasing the weight of the arrows.
    D. Increasing the parabolic path of the arrows.

78. Some students practicing basketball are having difficulty with "free throws" even though the shots make it to and over the hoop. What adjustment will improve their "free throws"?

    A. Increasing the height of release (i.e. jump shot).
    B. Increasing the vertical path of the ball.
    C. Increasing the velocity of the release.
    D. Increasing the base of support.

79. An archery student's arrow bounced off the red part of the target face. What is the correct ruling?

    A. No score.
    B. Re-shoot arrow.
    C. 7 points awarded.
    D. Shot receives same score as highest arrow shot that did not bounce off the target.

80. A student playing badminton believed that the shuttlecock was going to land out-of-bounds. The shuttlecock landed on the line. What is the correct ruling?

    A. The shuttlecock is out-of-bounds.
    B. The shuttlecock is in-bounds.
    C. The point is replayed.
    D. That player is charged with a feint.

81. A mechanical pinsetter accidentally knocked down the only bowling pin left standing for a spare attempt after clearing all the other pins knocked down by the first ball thrown. What is the correct ruling?

    A. Foul
    B. Spare
    C. Frame is replayed
    D. No count for that pin

82. The ball served in racquetball hits the front line and lands in front of the short line. What is the ruling?

    A. Fault
    B. Reserve
    C. Out-of-bounds
    D. Fair ball

83. Two opposing soccer players are trying to gain control of the ball when one player "knees" the other. What is the ruling?

    A. Direct free kick
    B. Indirect free kick
    C. Fair play
    D. Ejection from game

84. Two students are playing badminton. When receiving the shuttlecock, one student consistently stands too deep in the receiving court. What strategy should the server use to serve the shuttlecock?

    A. Smash serve
    B. Clear serve
    C. Overhead serve
    D. Short serve

85. A basketball team has an outstanding rebounder. In order to keep this player near the opponent's basket, which strategy should be implemented?

    A. Pick-and-Roll
    B. Give-and-Go
    C. Zone defense
    D. Free-lancing

86. When a defensive tennis player needs more time to return to his/her position, what strategy should be applied?

    A. Cross-court shot
    B. Dink shot
    C. Lob shot
    D. Down-the-line shot

87. An overhead badminton stroke used to hit a fore-hand-like overhead stroke which is on the backhand side of the body is called:

    A. Around-the-head-shot
    B. Down-the-line shot
    C. Lifting the shuttle
    D. Under hand shuttle

88. A maneuver when an offensive player passes to a teammate and then immediately cuts in toward the basket for a return pass is:

    A. Charging
    B. Pick
    C. Give-and-go
    D. Switching

89. A bowling pin that remains standing after an apparently perfect hit is called:

    A. Tap
    B. Turkey
    C. Blow
    D. Leave

90. A soccer pass from the outside of the field near the end line to a position in front of the goal is called:

    A. Chip
    B. Settle
    C. Through
    D. Cross

91. A volleyball that is simultaneously contacted above the net by opponents and momentarily held upon contact is called a/an:

    A. Double fault
    B. Play over
    C. Overlap
    D. Held ball

92. Volleyball player LB on team A digs a spiked ball. The ball deflects off of LB's shoulder. What is the ruling?

    A. Fault
    B. Legal hit
    C. Double foul
    D. Play over

93. A teacher who modifies and develops tasks for a class is demonstrating knowledge of which appropriate behavior in physical education activities?

    A. Appropriate management behavior
    B. Appropriate student behavior
    C. Appropriate administration behavior
    D. Appropriate content behavior

94. To enhance skill and strategy performance for striking or throwing objects, for catching or collecting objects, and for carrying and propelling objects, students must first learn techniques for:

    A. Offense
    B. Defense
    C. Controlling objects
    D. Continuous play of objects

95. Which of the following is not a type of tournament?

    A. Spiderweb
    B. Pyramid
    C. Spiral
    D. Round Robin

96. Which of the following is not a type of meet?

    A. Extramural
    B. Intramural
    C. Interscholastic
    D. Ladder

97. An instructor used a similar movement from a skill learned in a different activity to teaching a skill for a new activity. The technique used to facilitate cognitive learning was:

    A. Conceptual thinking
    B. Transfer of learning
    C. Longer instruction
    D. Appropriate language

98. A teacher rewards students' completion of tasks. Which method is used to facilitate psychomotor learning?

    A. Task/Reciprocal
    B. Command/Direct
    C. Contingency/Contract
    D. Physical/Reflex

99. All of the following are Systematic Observational Evaluations except:

    A. Reflective Recording
    B. Event Recording
    C. Duration Recording
    D. Self Recording

100. The ability for a muscle(s) to repeatedly contract over a period of time is:

    A. Cardiovascular endurance
    B. Muscle endurance
    C. Muscle strength
    D. Muscle force

101. The ability to rapidly change the direction of the body is:

    A. Coordination
    B. Reaction time
    C. Speed
    D. Agility

102. Students are performing the vertical jump. What component of fitness is being assessed?

    A. Muscle strength
    B. Balance
    C. Power
    D. Muscle endurance

103. Students are performing trunk extensions. What component of fitness is being assessed?

    A. Balance
    B. Flexibility
    C. Body Composition
    D. Coordination

104. Working at a level that is above normal is which exercise training principle?

    A. Intensity
    B. Progression
    C. Specificity
    D. Overload

105. Students on a running program to improve cardiorespiratory fitness are applying which exercise principle?

    A. Aerobic
    B. Progression
    C. Specificity
    D. Overload

106. Adding more reps to a set of weight lifting applies which exercise principle?

    A. Anaerobic
    B. Progression
    C. Overload
    D. Specificity -

107. Which of the following does not modify overload?

    A. Frequency
    B. Perceived exertion
    C. Time
    D. Intensity

108. Using the Karvonean Formula, compute the THR for a 16 year old student with a RHR of 60.

    A 122-163 beats per minute
    B. 130-168 beats per minute
    C. 142-170 beats per minute
    D. 146-175 beats per minute

109. Using Cooper's Formula, compute the THR for a 15 year old student.

    A. 120- 153 beats per minute
    B. 123-164 beats per minute
    C. 135-169 beats per minute
    D. 147-176 beats per minute

110. Prior to activity, students perform a 5-10 minute warm-up. Which is not recommended as part of the warm-up?

    A. Using the muscles that will be utilized in the following activity.
    B. Using a gradual aerobic warm-up.
    C. Using a gradual anaerobic warm-up.
    D. Stretching the major muscle groups to be used in the activity.

111. Which is not a benefit of warming up?

    A. Releasing hydrogen from myoglobin.
    B. Reducing the risk of musculoskeletal injuries.
    C. Using a gradual anaerobic warm-up.
    D. Stretching the major muscle groups to be used in the activity.

112. Which is not a benefit of cooling down?

    A. Preventing dizziness.
    B. Redistributing circulation.
    C. Removing lactic acid.
    D. Removing myoglobin.

113. Activities to specifically develop cardiovascular fitness must be:

    A. Performed without developing an oxygen debt.
    B. Performed twice daily.
    C. Performed every day.
    D. Performed for a minimum of 10 minutes.

114. Overloading for muscle strength includes all of the following except:

    A. Lifting heart rate to an intense level.
    B. Lifting weights every other day.
    C. Lifting with high resistance and low reps.
    D. Lifting 60% to 90% of assessed muscle strength.

115. Which of the following applies to progression?

    A. Begin stretching program every day.
    B. Begin stretching program with 3 sets of reps.
    C. Begin stretching program with ballistic stretching.
    D. Begin stretching program holding stretches for 15 seconds.

116. Which of following overload principles does not apply to begin improving body composition?

    A. Aerobic exercise three times per week.
    B. Aerobic exercise at a low intensity.
    C. Aerobic exercise for about an hour.
    D. Aerobic exercise in intervals of high intensity.

117. Which of the following principles of progression applies to improving muscle endurance?

    A. Lifting weights every day.
    B. Lifting weights at 20% to 30% of assessed muscle strength.
    C. Lifting weights with low resistance and low reps.
    D. Lifting weights starting at 60% of assessed muscle strength.

118. Which skill or health related components of fitness is not developed by aerobic dance?
    A. Cardiorespiratory
    B. Body composition
    C. Coordination
    D. Flexibility

119. Rowing develops which health or skill related component of fitness?

    A. Muscle endurance
    B. Flexibility
    C. Balance
    D. Reaction time

120. Calisthenics develops the following health and skill related components of fitness except:

    A. Muscle strength
    B. Body composition
    C. Power
    D. Agility

121. Which health or skill related components of fitness is developed by rope jumping?

    A. Balance
    B. Coordination
    C. Flexibility
    D. Muscle strength

122. Swimming does not improve which health or skill related component of fitness?

    A. Cardiorespiratory
    B. Flexibility
    C. Muscle strength
    D. Speed

123. Data from a cardiorespiratory assessment can identify and predict all of the following except:

    A. Functional aerobic capacity
    B. Natural overfatness
    C. Running ability
    D. Motivation

124. Data from assessing _____ identifies an individual's potential of developing musculoskeletal problems and an individual's potential of performing activities of daily living.

    A. Flexibility
    B. Muscle endurance
    C. Muscle strength
    D. Motor performance

125. A 17-year old male student performed 20 sit-ups, ran a mile in 8 minutes, and has a body fat composition of 17%. Which is the best interpretation of his fitness level?

    A. Average muscular endurance, good cardiovascular endurance; appropriate body fat composition.
    B. Low muscular endurance, average cardiovascular endurance; high body fat composition.
    C. Low muscular endurance, average cardiovascular endurance; appropriate body fat composition.
    D. Low muscular endurance, low cardiovascular endurance; appropriate body fat composition.

126. Based on the above information what changes would you recommend to improve this person's level of fitness?

    A. Muscle endurance training and cardiovascular endurance training.
    B. Muscle endurance training, cardiovascular endurance training, and reduction of caloric intake.
    C. Muscle strength training and cardiovascular endurance training.
    D. No changes necessary.

127. An obese student's fitness assessments were poor for every component of fitness. Which would you recommend first?

    A. A jogging program.
    B. A weight lifting program.
    C. A walking program.
    D. A stretching program.

128. Which of the following body types is the most capable of motor performance involving endurance?

    A. Endomorph
    B. Ectomorph
    C. Mesomorph
    D. Metamorph

129. Which is not a sign of stress?

    A. Irritability
    B. Assertiveness
    C. Insomnia
    D. Stomach problems

130. Which is not a common negative stressor?

    A. Loss of significant other.
    B. Personal illness or injury.
    C. Moving to a new state.
    D. Landing a new job.

131. Which is a negative coping strategy for dealing with stress?

   A. Recreational diversions
   B. Active thinking
   C. Alcohol use
   D. Imagery

132. The most important nutrient the body require, without which life can only be sustained for a few days, is:

   A. Vitamins
   B. Minerals
   C. Water
   D. Carbohydrates

133. With regard to protein content, foods from animal sources are usually:

   A. Complete
   B. Essential
   C. Nonessential
   D. Incidental

134. Fats with room for two or more hydrogen atoms per molecule-fatty acid chain are called:

   A. Monounsaturated
   B. Polyunsaturated
   C. Hydrounsaturated
   D. Saturated

135. An adequate diet to meet nutritional needs is:

   A. No more than 30% caloric intake from fats, no more than 50 % caloric intake from proteins, and at least 20% caloric intake from carbohydrates.
   B. No more than 30% caloric intake from fats, no more than 40% caloric intake from proteins, and at least 30% caloric intake from carbohydrates.
   C. No more than 30% caloric intake from fats, no more than 15% caloric intake from proteins, and at least 55% caloric intake from carbohydrates.
   D. No more than 30 % caloric intake from fats, no more than 30% caloric intake from proteins, and at least 40% caloric intake from carbohydrates.

136. Maintaining body weight is best accomplished by:

   A. Dieting
   B. Aerobic exercise
   C. Lifting weights
   D. Equalizing caloric intake to output

137. High protein diets:

   A. Are high in cholesterol
   B. Are high in saturated fats
   C. Require vitamin and mineral supplements
   D. All of the above

138. Which one of the following statements about low calorie diets is false?

   A. Most people who "diet only" regain the weight they lose.
   B. They are the way most people try to lose weight.
   C. They make weight control easier.
   D. They lead to excess worry about weight, food, and eating.

139. Which of the following health risk factors cannot be impoved by physical activity?

   A. Cholesterol levels
   B. Metabolic rate
   C. Stress related disorders
   D. Heart diseases

140. Physiological benefits of exercise include all of the following except:

   A. Reducing mental tension
   B. Improving muscle strength
   C. Cardiac hypertrophy
   D. Quicker recovery rate

141. Psychological benefits of exercise include all of the following except:

   A. Improved sleeping patterns
   B. Improved energy regulation
   C. Improved appearance
   D. Improved quality of life

142. This exercise improves which muscle group?

   A. Trapezius
   B. Deltoids
   C. Pectorals
   D. Latissimus dorsi

143. This exercise improves which muscle group?

A. Obliques
B. Abdominals
C. Biceps
D. Triceps

144. This exercise improves which muscle group?

A. Quadriceps
B. Abductors
C. Adductors
D. Gluteus

145. This exercise improves which muscle group?

A. Trapezius
B. Deltoids
C. Pectorals
D. Latissimus dorsi

146. This exercise improves which muscle group?

A. Obliques
B. Abdominals
C. Biceps
D. Triceps

147. This exercise improves which muscle group?

A. Quadriceps
B. Hamstrings
C. Abductors
D. Gluteus

148. Which of the following conditions is not associated with a lack of physical activity?

A. Atherosclerosis
B. Longer life expectancy
C. Osteoporosis
D. Certain cancers

149. Which is not an exercise myth or gimmick?

A. Muscle will turn into fat.
B. Children do not need to exercise.
C. Spot reduction is effective.
D. Pregnant women should exercise.

150. Which of the following exercise equipment is best for applying the physiological principles?

A. Rolling machines
B. Electrical muscle stimulators
C. Stationary bicycle
D. Motor-driven rowing machine